Reading Activities
for
Child Involvement

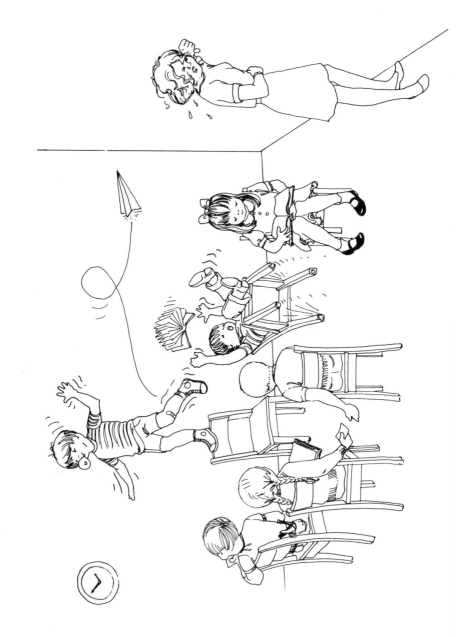

Reading Activities
for
Child Involvement

EVELYN B. SPACHE

Assistant Professor of Education,
Jacksonville University,
Jacksonville, Florida

ALLYN AND BACON, Inc.   **Boston**

Library of Congress Catalog Card Number:
71–182302

CONTENTS

PREFACE ix

INTRODUCTION 1

WHY THE NEED FOR THIS BOOK?, 1; WHAT THIS BOOK CON-
TAINS, 2; HOW TO USE THIS BOOK, 3.

One. TEACHER-MADE READING KITS 5

Rationale, 5; What Kind of Kit?, 6; Directions for Assem-
bly, 7; Color Coding, 7; Skill Box, 8; SUGGESTED MATERIALS
FOR KITS, 10.

Two. READING READINESS 13

I. VISUAL SKILLS: 13. Rationale, 13; Binocular Skills, 14;
Ocular Motility, 15; Visual Memory, 17. II. VISUAL-MOTOR
SKILLS: 18. Rationale, 18; Bodily Coordination, 19; Hand-
Eye Coordination, 21. III. VISUAL DISCRIMINATION SKILLS: 28.
Rationale, 28; Form Discrimination, 29; Letter Formation,

32; Word and Letter Discrimination, 33; Colors, 34. IV.
AUDITORY SKILLS: 35. Rationale, 35; Listening, Auditory
Memory, Auditory Discrimination, 36.

Three.   BASIC READING SKILLS   39

I. LETTER AND WORD RECOGNITION: 39. Rationale, 39; Own
Name, Numbers, Letters, Matching Letters, Capitals, Lowercase, Knowledge of the Alphabet, 44; Word Configuration,
Matching Words and Phrases, Compound Words, Word Recognition, 44. II. CONCEPTS OF READING: 56. Rationale, 56;
Directional Orientation to Pictures and Books, 57; Action
and Events Move Sequentially from Picture to Picture or
Page to Page, 57; Telling, Interpreting and Relating Stories
and Pictures, 58. III. COMPOSING OWN STORIES AND EXPERI-
ENCE CHARTS: 60. Rationale, 60; Dictated Stories, 61; Creative Writing, 63.

Four.   WORD PERCEPTION   65

I. PHONICS: 65. Rationale, 65; Phonic Syllabus, 67; Initial
Consonants, 68; Blends and Consonant Digraphs, 80; Short
and Long Vowels, 88; Blending Sounds into Words, 91;
Silent Letters, 94; Vowel Digraphs and Diphthongs, 96;
Controlled R, 99; Three- and Four-Letter Phonograms, 100;
Final Consonants, 108. II. STRUCTURAL ANALYSIS: 111. Ra-
tionale, 111; Contractions, 111; Plurals, 112; Word Struc-
ture, 113; Accent, 114; Roots, Prefixes, Suffixes, 115. III.
SYLLABICATION: 122. Rationale, 122; Syllabication Syllabus,
123; Division of Syllables, 124. IV. CONTEXTUAL ANALYSIS:
126. Rationale, 126; Idea Clues—Pictures, Experience (In-
ference), Comparison and Contrast, 127; Sentence Structure
—Word Position, Figures of Speech, Words Used as Noun,
Verb (Word Functions), 131.

**Five.   LANGUAGE DEVELOPMENT AND
VOCABULARY   135**

I. ORAL COMMUNICATION: 135. Rationale, 135; Communication—Group Activities, Individual Activities, 136; Interpretation, 137; Fluency, Inflection, 137. II. BUILDING SIGHT AND

MEANING VOCABULARY: 138. Rationale, 138; Categorizing and
Classifying Words, 139; Homonyms, Synonyms, Antonyms,
147; Multiple Meanings of Words and Usage, 150; Qualifying or Descriptive Words, 157.

Six.   **LOCATION SKILLS**   **160**

Rationale, 160. I. DICTIONARY SKILLS: 161. Alphabetic Se-
quence and Approximate Place of Letter in Alphabet (e.g.,
Middle or Last Quarter), 161; Alphabetizing by First Letter,
First Two or Three, 164; Ability to Interpret Guide Words,
166; Ability to Interpret Pronunciation Key, 166; Ability to
Comprehend Definitions, 167; Ability to Try Several Defini-
tions in Context, 168; Usage Terms and Abbreviations, 169.
II. LIBRARY SKILLS: 169. Table of Contents, 169; Card Cata-
log, 170; Reference Books, 170; Index, 172; Projects in
Finding Resource Materials for Reports, 174.

Seven.   **CONTENT READING SKILLS**   **176**

Rationale, 176. I. MAP AND GLOBE SKILLS: 177. Ability to
Orient Oneself in Relation to the Immediate Environment of
the Classroom, School and Community, 177; Reading a Map
According to Cardinal Directions, 178; Finding General Di-
rections on a Map or Globe, 178; Recognizing Scale and
Distance on Maps, 179; Locating Places on Maps and
Globes, 180; Understanding and Expressing Relative Loca-
tion of School Grounds and Community Buildings; Inter-
preting the Effects of Locations (such as Physical Features
of the Areas, Trade Routes and Climate), 180; Reading
and Using Map Symbols, Key or Legend, 181; Comparing
Maps and Drawing Inferences, 182. II. READING GRAPHS AND
CHARTS: 183. Making, Using and Interpreting Pictorial
Charts, 183; Making Circle Graphs to Show Child's Daily
Program, 183; Using and Making Bar Graphs, 184; Making
Time Lines to Show Chronology, 185. III. READING TABLES:
186. Interpreting and Making Simple Tables from Common
Sources, 186.

**Eight.   COMPREHENSION AND
             INTERPRETATION SKILLS   187**

Rationale, 187. I. UNDERSTANDING WHAT IS READ: 188. Selecting Title for Story, 188; Locating and Remembering Details
and Facts, 188; Following Written Directions, 192; Drawing
Conclusions, 196. II. INTERPRETATION THROUGH SHARING:
200. Dramatization, 200; Art Activities, 202; Book Reviews,
204; Character Analysis, 205. III. RATE IMPROVEMENT: 207.
Speed, 207; Skimming and Scanning, 208. IV. ORGANIZING
SKILLS: 209. Separating Fact from Fiction (Exaggerations),
209; Finding Irrelevant Parts, Sorting Related Statements,
210; Organization of Paragraph—Topic and Summary Sentences, 211; Time, Cause-Effect, 212; Sequence of Events,
213; Writing Brief Summaries (Stories or Paragraphs),
216; Outlining, 216.

Nine.   TIDBITS AND LEFTOVERS   221

CROSS-INDEX OF ACTIVITIES   233

PREFACE

The uniqueness of this collection of 571 activities to reinforce reading skills lies in the rationale presented as an introduction to each skill area. The rationales explain: 1) why the skill needs to be reinforced, 2) how to understand the skill and 3) what the child should be able to do (behaviorally stated) after completing the activities.

The activities are so arranged that users may find reinforcement at their fingertips, through the Cross-Index of Activities.

There is no valid reason for our children to learn reading skills through the "3D" method (Dull-Dry-Drill). Reading *can* be, and *should* be, stimulating and interesting.

The assistance of the many teachers in Jacksonville, Florida in trying the activities in their classrooms, and in furnishing the author with teacher and child reactions, is greatly appreciated.

I am deeply grateful to my husband, Dr. George D. Spache, Professor Emeritus, University of Florida, for his support and assistance. Also, to Judy Crumley, whose creative ideas are exceeded only by her excellence in classroom teaching, for her aid in organizing material and drawing the illustrations.

Evelyn B. Spache
Sarasota, Florida

Reading Activities
for
Child Involvement

INTRODUCTION

WHY THE NEED FOR THIS BOOK?

Teaching a skill or a concept by means of a directed lesson is merely a preliminary step to the actual learning of the skill or concept by the child. The learning takes place *only* when the student reinforces this skill by using it in interesting, meaningful situations. Unless the directed lesson is followed by this reinforcement, future use of the skill may not be realized.

Basic reader teacher's manuals offer excellent guides to teaching skills, but teachers often voice a desire for follow-up ideas and activities to ensure learning. The activities offered herein are specifically designed to reinforce the basic reading skills of any reading program. They were carefully chosen for: 1) child interest; 2) availability of materials; 3) ease of directions; 4) variety, and 5) depth of thinking involved.

The same philosophy of meeting individual differences that is evident in *Reading in the Elementary School*, by Spache and Spache (Allyn and Bacon, 1969), is present throughout these activities. The arrangement is such that the activities correlate with the concepts developed in the textbook. However, they are relevant, of course, to any reading program.

1

WHAT THIS BOOK CONTAINS

Organization—Each new skill area is prefaced by a Rationale. The rationale explains why the teaching or reinforcing of the skills should be developed. The teacher should have a clear concept of why the skill is stressed (or not stressed), and how it is to be put to use.

The Behavioral Outcomes are consistent with the concept that what is learned should be evident to the learner and readily observable by the teacher. Thus, the behavioral outcomes describe what the child can consciously do and what the teacher can watch him do.

Interspersed with the activities are numerous "Hints" to the teacher. These are ideas that teachers have found useful in any approach to reading. Many have been offered by our fellow teachers.

The activities are purposely not labeled by grade or age level. We feel that many of the activities for primary children can also be useful to intermediate students who are reading at much lower levels. Likewise, many advanced reading skills can be emphasized at primary levels. Therefore, activities within each skill area are arranged according to difficulty, from very simple to sophisticated; not by grade levels.

In some instances, only a few changes in words or in directions are necessary to make the exercise easier or more challenging, as the teacher desires.

Use of Materials—Throughout this book we have specified use of the overhead projector, chalkboard, charts, films and, particularly, acetate folders and markers. When one of these aids is not available, we assume the teacher will utilize another means of presentation.

We have very positive feelings concerning the acetate folders (page protectors). They allow the teacher to use printed or duplicated material again and again, without rewriting on the board or duplicating on paper. Your time and energies are important, and should be conserved wisely in this fashion.

There is a second justification for the use of acetate folders. School should be a place where children can make mistakes comfortably. Using the suggested acetate folders (*see* Teacher-Made Kits), the student can wipe away errors and make a fresh start, with ease and without embarrassment. This is a tremendous aid in building positive self-concepts.

A real attempt has been made to give clear directions for constructing games and activities. The suggested materials are usually available from school supplies or from local business establishments (often free), such as printers, milk companies or construction companies.

We urge that children construct the games whenever possible. This, in itself, is functional practice in following directions and in visual-motor coordination.

HOW TO USE THIS BOOK

1. Try to become familiar with all of the activities. Make notes in the margins, underline and star ideas you think particularly useful.

2. Observe your students carefully as they work, to diagnose or detect their weaknesses in skill development.

3. Prescribe activities to fit needs. Use the cross-index for variety and depth in skill development exercises.

4. Be sure the child is aware of his need, and knows how this activity or game will help him improve. The Behavioral Outcomes will help both you and the pupil judge his progress.

5. Do not hesitate to put this book in the hands of the children. Many intermediate level students are capable of reading and following the directions by themselves. Instructing others in the procedures of play helps to develop leadership ability.

Chapter One

TEACHER-MADE READING KITS

Rationale

In order to meet individual differences in skill development it is necessary that the teacher have readily available materials on many levels which cover a wide variety of skills. The teacher-made kit is a most valuable asset to beginning teachers. Equipped with her skill box, she can begin meeting individual needs immediately, even if the school supplies are late, or as is often the case, if they do not meet the needs of her students.

Teacher-made kits are, naturally, less expensive than commercial kits. They can be made to fill particular needs, and can be expanded as needed.

Of all materials used in schools, workbooks are probably the most misused. The inexperienced or naive teacher may order a particular skill book and expect all students to work through it simultaneously, regardless of the reading level of the child or his particular skill needs. The teacher-made kit makes use of the best of these workbooks in a manner that puts them in the hands of the student when he most needs that particular material.

What Kind of Kit?

Word attack? Comprehension? Vocabulary? Or fun and games? Many teachers feel insecure in teaching word attack skills. Their college courses may have been particularly weak in this area. Therefore, these teachers would probably feel more secure in beginning with a word attack kit and developing additional kits as needed.

Other teachers, secure in this area, may feel the need of kits in different areas because of particular strengths or weaknesses, availability of materials or student needs.

Selection of Workbooks

We strongly suggest these steps in the selection of materials:

1. Purchase several workbooks emphasizing one major skill area, each at a different grade level.
2. Select workbooks in which there is a clear indication of the nature of each skill at the top of each page.
3. Choose workbooks which offer only one major skill per page.
4. Try to secure workbooks which give simple and obvious directions at the top of each page.

Supplies Needed to Assemble Kit:

two copies of student workbooks

one copy of teacher's edition for self-correction

*$8\frac{1}{2}\times11$ cardboards or oaktag (shirt cardboards from a laundry are perfect!)

acetate folders OR materials for laminating with drymount press

masking tape

colored mystic tape

wax base markers (crayons or grease pencils)

water-soluble markers (pens or pencils)

attractively decorated box

* *Note:* 9×12 cardboard may be used if you laminate. If using acetate folders, this size would be too large.

Directions for Assembly:

1. Remove staples from workbook.
2. Cut the workbook down center back.
3. Separate pages of all workbooks into different piles for each skill.
4. Place odd-numbered pages from one workbook on one side of the tagboard, and even-numbered pages from second workbook on reverse side.
5. Seal each page to board all around the edges with masking tape.

Color Coding:

1. Choose a different color for each SKILL. Draw a magic marker across top of page, giving a solid line of color. Mystic tape may be used if preferred. If tape is used, overlap it to other side, coding both sides at once.

Suggested code for skills:

Red		initial consonants
Red ⋯	(red dots)	final and medial consonants
Orange		consonant blends and digraphs
Yellow		short vowels
Green		long vowels
Blue		vowel digraphs and diphthongs
Purple		structural analysis
Brown		alphabetical order
Black		other skills (compounds, contractions, opposites)

2. Choose a different color for each LEVEL.

3. Mark the corner of the sheet with the chosen color to indicate level of difficulty. Each sheet is now coded with two colors: one for SKILL, another for LEVEL.

4. Suggested color code for levels:

Primer   black

1   red

2   orange

3   yellow

4   green

5   purple

Jr. Hi   brown

Sr. Hi   black

5. Place these completed sheets in acetate page protectors. If these are not available, single acetates (transparencies) may be clipped on when needed. (You may want to place Scotch tape across the bottom to prevent the sheet from sliding out.)

OR

Run entire sheet through laminating process.

6. File sheets in prepared box, grouping skill-coded sheets by sections.

7. Place teachers' editions in rear of box.

Skill box

1. Choose any grocery store box that will hold the sheets upright for easy viewing.

2. Cut down one side for easy removal and refiling of sheets.

3. Cover box with contact paper, or enamel paint.

4. Place card with skill code on front or side of box to assist students in refiling sheets.

Examples:

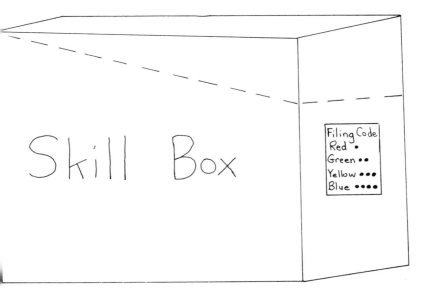

Variations:

Kits may be made for many types of activities. *Comprehension kits* are popular, using an arrangement similar to the above:

red	Sequence
orange	Context clues
yellow	Main idea
blue	Getting facts
purple	Following directions
black	Dictionary skills, etc.

Vocabulary kits, using crossword and other paper and pencil puzzles, are excellent. Coding is not necessary for these kits, but will be helpful if several levels of difficulty are included. Be sure to have answer keys available for self-correction.

Tips

1. The *simplest* arrangement is merely to place the workbook sheets in the acetate envelope and file it. However, these sheets lack *body* and will not stand up in the file box. Also, they are more inclined to slide off desks onto the floor and become scratched.

2. *Marking pens*—choose these with care! When shopping, take an acetate with you to try various brands of markers. Make sure they have *water soluble* ink and fine tips. See that they do not "bead," but make clear, firm lines. Check to see that a piece of dampened sponge or Nu-Von will easily remove marks.

    Wax or plastic base markers—1) Grease pencils are usable but a point is difficult to maintain. Also, primary children are apt to unravel them. 2) Crayons work well but you will need small pencil sharpeners to keep a good point. 3) Plastic markers (Ideal) are excellent. All of these are easily erased with dry Nu-Von or a facial tissue. 4) Transparency pencils of some types often give excellent results.

3. *Storing Markers*—A smaller, matching box may be placed inside the front of the kit to hold marking materials.

Conclusion

Kits can be made from various materials for a multiplicity of purposes. Your creative ideas alone set the limits. The basic rationale is to give the student the proper skill sheets *when* he *needs* them.

SUGGESTED MATERIALS FOR KITS

Perceptual Kit

Continental Press: *Visual Readiness Skills—Levels 1 and 2; Seeing Likenesses and Differences—Levels 1, 2 and 3; Visual-Motor Skills— Levels 1 and 2.*

Word Recognition and Vocabulary

Dolch Puzzle Book, I and II (I—easy half; II—harder half).

IMED Publishers: *Crossword Puzzles for Word Power*—Starter Books 1 and 2; Books 1-3.

Grosset and Dunlap: Treasure Books Division, *Crossword Puzzle Series: Crossword Puzzles*—Grades 2-6; *Famous People*, 5-6; *Animal Crossword Puzzles*, 4-5; *Old Testament*, 4-5; *New Testament*, 4-5; *Fairy Tales*, 3-4; *Sports Heroes*, 4-5; *Great Americans*, 4-5; *Great Inventions*, 4-5. Scholastic—*Scope–Word Skills*, 1 and 2.

Word Analysis

American Education Publications: *Phonics and Word Power*, Programs 1-3.

Educator's Publisher: *Primary Phonics*, Workbook 1, and other phonics materials.

Lyons and Carnahan: *Phonics We Use*, Primer to Grade 6 (Books A-G).

McCormick-Mathers: *Speedboat*, etc.

Merrill: *Phonics Skill Textbooks*, A-D.

Modern Curriculum Press: *Phonics Is Fun*, Readiness Books 1 and 2.

Comprehension and Study Skills

Allyn and Bacon: Sheldon Series—*Activity Books*, 4-6 (especially strong in study and location skills, graphs, maps, etc.).

American Education Publications: *My Weekly Reader* Practice Books—*Map Skills*, 2-6; *Science Reading Adventures*, 1-6; *Read-Study-Think*, 1-6.

Barnell-Loft: Specific Skill Series—1-6, *Using the Context, Working with Sounds, Getting the Facts, Locating the Answer, Following Directions.*

Continental Press: *Reading-Thinking Skills*, 1-6.

Lippincott Company: *Reading for Meaning Workbooks*—Grades 4, 5, 6.

Merrill: *Diagnostic Reading Workbooks*, 1-6; *Nip the Bear*—1; *Red Deer, Indian Boy*—2; *Scottie and His Friends*—3; *Adventure Trails*—4; *Exploring Today*—5; *Looking Ahead*—6.

Merrill: *Reading Skill Texts*, Grades 1-6; *Bibs*—Grade 1; *Nicky*—2; *Uncle Funny Bunny*—3; *Uncle Ben*—4; *Tom Trott*—5; *Pat the Pilot* —6.

Reader's Digest: *Reading Skill Builders* and Practice Pads 1-6.

Webster: *New Practice Readers*, Books A, B, C; 1, 2, 3 (Grades 2-6).

Chapter Two

READING READINESS

I. VISUAL SKILLS

Rationale

About half the children who enter the first grade cannot control their eyes sufficiently to follow a line of objects or printed words. They do not have enough two-eyed coordination to look sequentially along a line of images. One or both of their eyes tend to wander away from the pictures or words they are trying to look at. Yet, the reading act demands a high degree of binocular control in maintaining attention on a line from left to right. Without good binocular coordination, even keeping the place on the line is very difficult, not to mention learning to read accurately.

BEHAVIORAL OUTCOMES

The child will learn:

> to maintain fixation on a moving object
> to follow a moving object with his eyes
> to move easily from point to point with his eyes

to maintain stable fixation on an object while moving

to maintain sequential fixation on a line of objects

Binocular Skills

1. Walking Beam*

Directions for constructing beam: The only material needed is a standard 2×4, about fourteen feet in length. Cut three eighteen-inch pieces from the board. These pieces will be the braces. The remaining footage (approximately ten feet) will be the walking beam.

Using a saw, cut the notches in each of the three braces, as shown. Place beam in four-inch notch for beginners. This is a very inexpensive and beneficial piece of equipment.

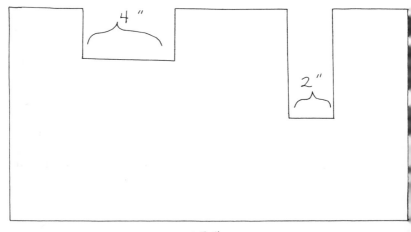

General instructions: Have a fixation target, such as X on the blackboard or a small picture, at eye level, opposite the end of the beam. Children should always look at this target when exercising on the beam.

* Adapted from *Readiness for Learning* by J. N. Getman, et al. St. Louis: Webster Publishing Co.

INDIAN WALK. Have children walk, Indian fashion, heel touching toe, along the beam. Keep eyes fixed on the target.

BUTTERFLY. Using the Indian walk, spread arms out like a butterfly, moving them up and down slowly, while moving along the beam.

BACKWARD WALK. Walk backward on the beam, toe and heel fashion. Keep eyes on the target.

BACKWARD BUTTERFLY. Walk backward on the beam, moving arms up and down slowly, like a butterfly.

FORWARD AND BACKWARD. Walk forward until teacher or other pupil says, "Stop," then reverse, moving backward. Use Indian walk, heel to toe, in each direction.

LEARNING DISTANCES. Put a red stripe across the beam at the middle, and green stripes at the one-quarter and three-quarter points. Use the forward and backward movements upon command, using the words "one-half," "one-quarter," "two-quarters" or "three-quarters."

PERIPHERAL TARGETS. Place the walking beam parallel to the wall or chalkboard. Position the beam about two feet from the wall. Put a red circle at the child's eye level, on the wall or board at a point opposite the halfway mark on the beam. Have children try to walk the beam, with arms extended to the side, until they think they are even with the red circle and can touch it, without looking in that direction. Repeat exercise with beam placed at an angle (forty-five degrees or less) to the wall. Again, have them try to touch the red circle without looking at it. Practice touching the side targets while walking backward as well as forward, as well as starting from either end of the beam.

Ocular Motility

2. This activity is helpful to relieve visual tension from doing near point work. Place four large cards, with one numeral on each card (1, 2, 3, 4), in the four corners of one side of the room that the children are facing. Two cards will be high, near the ceiling; two low, near the floor. Place cards as near the corners as possible. Each child has an index card or

BALANCE BEAM

NAME	4″ BEAM							2″ BEAM						
	INDIAN	BUTTERFLY	BACKWARD	BACKWARD BUTTERFLY	FORWARD & BACKWARD	DISTANCES	TARGETS	INDIAN	BUTTERFLY	BACKWARD	BACKWARD BUTTERFLY	FORWARD & BACKWARD	DISTANCES	TARGETS

folded sheet of paper. He places this edgewise to his nose so he can see two of the numbers with one eye, the other half of the room with the other eye (he may close one eye at a time to check this). With both eyes open, he looks at the numbers the teacher (or leader) calls, such as "1-3-4-2-3-1-4-3."

This activity causes the students to use both eyes independently at far point, relieving tiredness from working at desk level.

3. Swinging Ball. Suspend a small rubber ball (or any similar object) from a doorway, a light fixture or the hand, at the child's eye level.

Gently swing the ball to and fro, in a circle, and from side to side, a foot or two from his face, while he follows it with his eyes. To vary this exercise, hang the ball about three feet from the floor, and have the child watch it while lying directly beneath it. Or, have the child try to follow movement of ball with a jar four or five inches in diameter, without hitting sides of jar. This can be varied by asking child to reach out with his forefinger to touch the ball in flight, from beneath or the side.

Visual Memory

1. Finding the Missing Parts. The teacher may use pictures from old magazines, books or newspapers. Parts of the pictures are removed and the children are asked to locate the missing parts. For example, the teacher may cut the tail off the picture of a dog, or the engine off the picture of a train.

5. Word Recognition. Have students watch as you write a word on the board. Immediately erase the word and ask students to tell you the word that had been written on the board. As a variation, several sight words may be written and a child may come up and erase any word he knows.

6. To check visual perception try these exercises:
   A. Look at the back of the room, then answer these questions:

   1. What is on top of the bookcase?
   2. Name the color of the flower vase.
   3. What is in the center of the library table?

7. The teacher holds up a picture or draws a large symbol easily reproduced. The children look at the object for several seconds (about ten) and then try to reproduce it as accurately as possible. Show the original copy again, in order for students to see how well they drew the form.

8. Several objects are placed in a line and the children are told to look at them carefully. They close their eyes while the teacher or a child removes one from the line. The children try to guess the missing object. This device may also be used for order. The children are asked to remember the objects in order from left to right. While their eyes are closed, one child shifts the order of two or three objects, then someone is asked to replace them in correct left-to-right order.

9. Seeing Likenesses and Differences. Select three children to stand in front of the class. Give the others a chance to look them over for likenesses or differences. They may note hair color, clothing, Sally's bow, Fred's untied shoe, etc. The children leave the room and one child changes something about his appearance before returning. The class-mates reexamine the children and try to guess the difference.

10. Divide a square of heavy tagboard into sixteen squares. On one side letter from A through P, and on the other number from 1 through 16. Students study the positions of all letters and numbers. With the number side up, ask these quetsions:

> Which letter is behind 9?
> Which letter is behind 1?
> Which letter is behind 14?

The reverse may also be used. Score may be kept for two to four players.

II. VISUAL-MOTOR SKILLS

Rationale

Discrimination of the forms and shapes which constitute reading is based fundamentally upon the bodily hand and eye experiences of the child. Up-down, front-back, near-far and left-right discriminations are first learned in the muscles. Gradually, during the early years of life the child learns to translate the muscular cues of distance, size, directionality and shape into visual cues. He moves slowly from the circle to the cross, to the straight line, the square, the diagonal line, the diamond and other cues to size, directionality and the like. Only when this development is far advanced is the child ready to apply these visual cues in the act of reading. Many primary children have not reached this stage of development, as shown in their difficulties in reproducing forms, matching forms, attempting to draw common objects and trying to write letters.

Children will vary considerably in their needs for these training exercises. Some well-developed, highly coordinated children may be able to move through the exercises in a week or two. Other children will need much longer periods, perhaps extending into a number of months, before they achieve rapid, fluent hand-eye coordination and are really ready for success in reading.

Some children will be admitted to the basal reading program on the basis of their readiness test scores. Yet, they may still need this basic visual training for some time afterward. It is expected that teachers will continue to offer this training to these children until their chalkboard and near-point performances show that it is no longer needed.

BEHAVIORAL OUTCOMES

The child will learn:

to hold fixation while executing a variety of bodily movements

to execute directionality in coordinated hand-eye movements

to achieve rhythmic hand-eye movements

to recognize and execute common shapes by exercises with geometric forms

to make discriminations involving directionality, size, shape, distance, etc.

Bodily Coordination

11. The *balance disc* provides an independent activity for bodily coordination. The child maintains balance while: 1) moving feet from center to outside edges of disc, 2) raising one foot at a time, and 3) bending his knees, turning around or executing other movements.

The disc should be painted with a rough texture paint (add coarse sand), or nonslip rubber strips should be used (such as in bathtubs). You may wish to use the disc on a carpeted area or on heavy cardboard, so as to keep corners from bumping the floor.

Materials: a square or round piece of ⅝" plywood, approximately 18" diameter; one 2x4x1 piece wood (piece of 2x4 is good); epoxy; bolt and nut (about 2½").

Directions: With epoxy, adhere the 2x4 block to underside of plywood. Put bolt through block and plywood. Secure bolt on top. File off any

excess part of bolt. Place nonslip strips on top surface. This is very
simple to construct and costs less than one dollar for a wonderful piece
of balance equipment.

VARIATION: For students who are ready for further balance skills, add
an additional 2x4 block to underside. This is great fun.

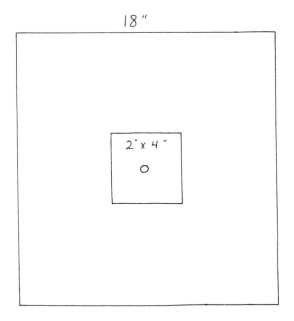

12. To develop awareness of the tactile sense, blindfold one child and
place an object in his hand, such as a pencil, pine cone, eraser or apple.
Ask him to identify the object only by touch.

FOLLOW-UP: When everyone has had a turn, have a child hold an object
in his hand so that the class cannot see it. As he describes how the object
feels, the class can guess what it is.

13. String colored beads or blocks (buttons may do). Knot the string
firmly.

Supply children with box of matching beads or blocks and shoestring
knotted at one end. Children string the beads in the same order as model.
Several pattern sequences should be used.

14. Children who have difficulty with writing may need small muscle
activities. Have several objects that require finger-thumb pressure such
as clothespins and lines, or cardboard with marks showing where to clip

OTHER ACTIVITIES:

Squeezing clay

Squeezing a small, soft ball

Making pegboard designs

Pushing in and pulling out thumbtacks or brads

Manipulating small blocks into patterns

Hand-Eye Coordination

CHALKBOARD ACTIVITIES*

General instructions: All chalkboard work is done with the child standing. He stands at a comfortable writing distance from the chalkboard. Center the chalkboard at the level of his nose. There is usually no problem of maintaining motivation, since the teacher must work right with the child. If a child ever finds some particular procedure too difficult for him, drop back to a simpler procedure. The basic rule is *never to advance the child too rapidly.* Give him a rest period if he exhibits motor fatigue. Training periods should not be longer than ten to fifteen minutes a day, but should occur daily.

Use a felt-tip marking pen to make patterns on chalkboard. These may be removed later with alcohol.

15. Unimanual Training Procedures

A. Make a vertical row of dots on the chalkboard at about ten inches to the right of the center position, and a similar row of dots to the left of the center position. Label each dot on the same horizontal line similarly; the vertical spacing between the dots should be about three inches. The pattern will look like this:

```
A   •                    •   A

B   •                    •   B

C   •                    •   C
```

* Adapted from work done by Dr. Leo Manas, who has used them extensively in his optometric practice.

About five pairs of dots are sufficient. The child is given his piece of chalk and holds it in his preferred hand. He places it on the dot by the letter **A** on his left. He then scribes a chalk line from the left **A** to the right **A** in a straight line, WITHOUT STOPPING. When he has completed drawing the lines, erase the lines, and have the child continue the training. If these lines can be drawn easily, continuously and accurately (start precisely from one dot and end right on the other dot), advance the child to procedure B.

B. Construct two rows of horizontal dots, with a vertical spacing of about twelve inches between each row. In the horizontal rows, the dots should be about three inches apart. The chalkboard pattern will now be:

```
        A   B   C   D   E

        •   •   •   •   •


        •   •   •   •   •

        A   B   C   D   E
```

The child is asked to start with his chalk at the dot below the letter **A** and draw a CONTINUOUS line to the lower **A**. This is done for all the different letters, so that he ends up with a series of vertical lines. Now, have the child reverse the procedure AND again make a series of vertical lines, starting with the lower dots and going upward to the higher dots. When the child can perform adequately on the horizontal and vertical lines, we advance to the oblique lines.

C. Again, two rows of dots are constructed and labeled but placed at an oblique angle:

Child scribes lines in a left-to-right downward direction. The dots can also be placed in the reverse pattern:

The child scribes from left to right, upward. The child must make a continuous line starting from one dot and ending at the other dot before we consider that he has developed adequate performance ability.

D (Combining straight and oblique lines). Using the rows of dots as in exercises A, B and C, ask the child to draw both horizontally (as in A) and obliquely, from the dot at the right to the second dot at the left:

E. Repeat, using the vertical spacing of dots, as in exercise B above, and the oblique spacing, as in C:

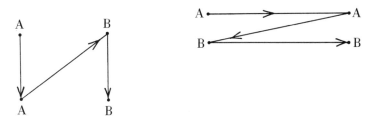

The child should make a continuous, rapid line from each dot to the next. *Note:* These lines are drawn straight, quickly and with a single free motion, NOT painstakingly slowly with only hand or wrist movement.

16. Repetitive Forms. This technique develops rhythm, shape or form, and the ability to maintain constancy of size. Two parallel lines are constructed across the board, about six inches apart, at the nose level of the child. He starts with his chalk about four inches from the left edge of the lines and makes circles in a counterclockwise direction, moving slowly toward the right as he scribes his circles. It looks as follows:

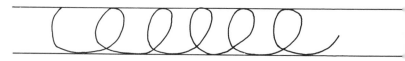

As a variation of this, have the child scribe vertical lines in the same manner.

These lines may be used later for practice in letter formation and spacing.

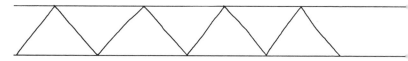

When the child can perform these visual-kinesthetic procedures with ease and accuracy, we proceed to "Chase the Leader."

"Chase the Leader." Construct a series of three or more dots on a chalkboard, and label them **A, B, C, . . . M.** The child must go in the proper direction, and continuously scribe a line from **A** to **B** and on to the last letter on the chalkboard. This teaches recognition of the letters of the alphabet in proper sequence, and develops ability to scribe lines rapidly in all directions; it teaches the child to be able to make a rapid shift in direction (to draw angles), and also enables him to develop the ability to stay on his primary target in spite of the distraction of other lines in the field of view. Start with three dots, then increase to five, seven or more.

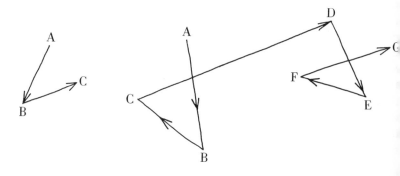

17. Bimanual Training Procedures

Bimanual circles. A fixation point, an **X,** is placed on the chalkboard at the nose level of the child. The child is moved to about ten inches from the chalkboard. He holds a piece of chalk in each hand and places the chalk in contact with the board at about one inch from the fixation point. The left chalk is one inch to the left of the fixation point, and the right chalk one inch to its right. The child starts upward with each hand, making a circle pattern on the board with each hand. The left hand is moving counterclockwise, and the right hand clockwise.

The child continues making the circles with both hands, trying to improve on the contour of the form to make a perfect circle.

These movements may be changed by having the left hand move clockwise and the right counterclockwise, or both hands moving in the same direction. Whenever the board gets filled with circles the board is erased and a new fixation point marked. The child then continues the bimanual circles procedures.

18. Bimanual Straight Lines.
The teacher places a large circle of dots on the blackboard or easel, with a large center dot at the height of the child's eyes. The dots around the circle are lettered or numbered; if the child cannot read these symbols, the teacher indicates the two dots for the starting points. The child then tries to draw with both hands, from two dots on opposite edges of the circle to the center dot, or the reverse, from the center to two opposite outer dots. Extend this training so that the child can draw simultaneously from any two dots to the center or the reverse. The lines should be drawn at once, straight and quickly, once the starting points have been identified. Dots scattered in any order on the blackboard, to be connected with straight lines, is a sound, unimanual extension of this type of exercise.

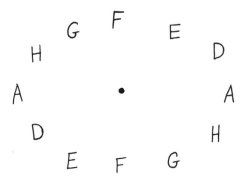

When all the chalkboard exercises have been completed satisfactorily, you may wish to repeat exercises on paper at the child's desk. The chalkboard training should make the child progress somewhat faster in the desk exercises. This near point training can go on simultaneously with other desk activities such as the Continental Press worksheets.

19. Template Training.* The templates are geometric forms cut out of 9x12 masonite boards or heavy cardboard. The cutout portion is about seven inches tall, off center, so that the child can hold onto the board comfortably with the nonwriting hand. Forms include the circle, square, triangle, rectangle and diamond. Templates containing smaller forms, all five, may be constructed for use at the desk.

Directions:

1. Child holds template against chalkboard with one hand, centered a little below his nose. He stands erect, about twelve to fifteen inches from the board.

2. With the chalk, the child traces clockwise inside the cutout, keeping the chalk against the edge. He scribes around and around, starting always at the top, while he or the teacher counts (to two for the circle, to three or four for the other forms).

3. Continue until child can trace the shape freely without breaks or deviations from the edge. Then, repeat entire procedure in counterclockwise direction.

4. When performance becomes smooth, let child try shape with writing hand without aid of template.

* Adapted from the suggestions of the *Teacher's Manual for Perceptual Training*, Winter Haven Lions Research Foundation, Box 1045, Winter Haven, Florida.

5. Use desk templates in same fashion, first clockwise then counterclockwise, with and without template. When forms are mastered, use different shapes to make designs and pictures.

Note: If the inside edges of the template are rough, bind the edges with mystic tape to provide a smoother surface.

20. Circle or Line Game. Children are given sheets of paper with circles or vertical lines arranged in groups of varying numbers. Each sheet has a green margin at the left. The children are asked to begin at the margin and draw a horizontal line through the center of each cluster of objects, being careful not to extend their line beyond the outside boundary of the objects. The teacher must be careful always to work from left to right in illustrating this method with children. If desired, the task may be timed occasionally to encourage speed and accuracy.

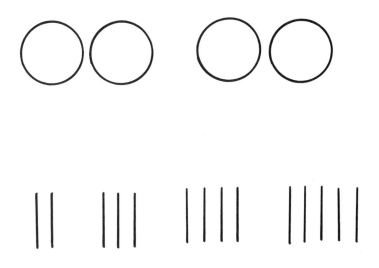

21. Making Puzzles. Mount a colorful picture on heavy cardboard or shirt cardboard. Cut it into pieces to make a jigsaw puzzle. Pieces may be kept together in an envelope. Each puzzle piece should bear the same number as the envelope, so that children will not mix up the puzzles. Children will enjoy putting the puzzle together and making up a story to accompany it.

22. Suspend a small rubber ball (3 to 4″ diameter) from a rod (a chart rack is good), so that it hangs at about the children's chest level. Two players bunt the ball back and forth to each other, using rolling pins; the wooden kitchen variety is best. To suspend the ball, staple a cord or yarn to the ball and hang from the rod.

23. Cut the bottom and one side (just below the handle) from a large bleach bottle. Use this for a mitt. Form a circle, with one child in the middle. Each child must have a mitt. Give the child in the center a small whiffle ball. He tosses the ball from his mitt to a child in the circle. That child catches it in his mitt and tosses it back.

24. Instructional Aid. Use a pegboard and pegs or a nailboard to reproduce geometric shapes and line designs. Colored yarn or rubber bands manipulate easily to form the patterns. Small cards showing patterns may be used; have the student reproduce the given design. This is also useful in creating original designs.

25. A small group makes a circle, one child in the center. The center child tosses a bean bag to another child. If it is caught it is tossed back to the center child; if missed, they exchange places.

26. Instructional Aid. On shirt cardboards, or other stiff paper, paint or color a large, simple design. With a hole-punch, perforate around the design. Children will develop visual-motor skills by outlining the design with yarn and a blunt needle or long bootlaces. A child must unlace a card before returning it to the box. Laces may be kept stuck into a sponge on a shelf, to prevent tangling.

27. Two teams are formed. The first persons are several feet from trash cans. Each child has a turn to toss a bean bag (eraser, sponge) into the container. Each team has a "retriever" who tosses the object to the next person in line.

This is an excellent rainy day activity.

III. VISUAL DISCRIMINATION SKILLS

Rationale

Progress in the continuum from muscular learning to visual learning must move toward the fine discriminations demanded by letters and words. This ability to read and write the symbols of reading, we call *visual discrimination.* Developmental stages include form discrimination first, with three-dimensional materials, and later, with paper and pencil in two-dimensional reproduction and matching. Shapes and forms are thus closely related to the hand-eye movements of writing and the visual movements of reading. Recognition of word shapes proceeds directly from the two- and three-dimensional experiences with other forms and shapes. Learning to write strengthens and reinforces the visual act of reading; only occasionally can children learn to read who cannot form letters accurately.

BEHAVIORAL OUTCOMES

The child will learn:

> to reproduce three-dimensional patterns and designs
>
> to reproduce or match two-dimensional objects or forms
>
> to recognize and reproduce letters
>
> to recognize word configurations

Form Discrimination

28. When discussing shapes, hold up a design and ask, "What do we see that is the same shape?" Many items will be in easy view.

29. Collect pictures which contain various fundamental shapes. Mount these on oaktag or stiff paper. Children will enjoy observing closely to see how many squares, circles or other shapes can be found in each picture.

30. Locating Similar Shapes. The teacher makes a set of various shapes, sizes or designs from construction paper. The children are given duplicate sets. They group these objects according to shape or color. Other classification devices may be used. The shapes (circles, hexagons, rectangles or others) and classification will vary according to the ability of your children.

31. A ditto sheet which is covered with squares may be given to the pupils. In each square, the children are instructed to draw something that is square in their classroom. The next day they illustrate things that are square which may be found outside; the next day, in a store, and so on. This would be a good way to introduce new shapes (circles, triangles or others) or, if desired, each child may be given different ones. At the end of the day or week, the children may share their ideas.

32. Each child in the group is given a geometric shape cut from colored construction paper. Squares, triangles, rectangles and circles may be used.

The teacher holds up a shape and asks, "If you have this shape, hold it up. What is the name of the shape? What can we see in our room that is this same shape? What other things do you know of that have this shape?" Continue with other shapes if attention-span warrants; otherwise, continue another time. The same idea may be used with colors.

FOLLOW-UP: Children may cut objects of the same shapes from magazines and paste on pages to make booklets or a large chart.

33. Make a large class spinner and a set of cards for each child in the group. Each set contains geometric shapes in color. Identical shapes appear on the spinner. As the spinner indicates a shape of a certain color, each child holds up his matching card.

34. Children may be given pictures of various vehicles. They may be asked to group or classify them according to vehicles that travel on land, air or water. Other types of pictures may be used, such as animals, clothing or foods. These may be classified by shape, size, number of legs, etc. The pictures may be mounted on charts for additional reinforcement.

35. The teacher may draw one or more lines on the board and see how many objects the students can make from them. After various ideas have been shared, she may give each child a sheet with pairs of parallel lines, in different sizes and slanted in different directions. The students fill in the lines and make pictures from them. This may be carried further by giving students sheets containing several circles, triangles, rectangles or other shapes and having the children make pictures from each object. Not only can this be done with lines and shapes, but also with letters.

36. Cut sixty 3″ square cards. Choose ten designs, and make six cards for each. Deal the cards out to four players (each gets 15 cards). The cards are placed facedown in front of each player. Each player turns over his top card so everyone can see it. If the child sees a card that

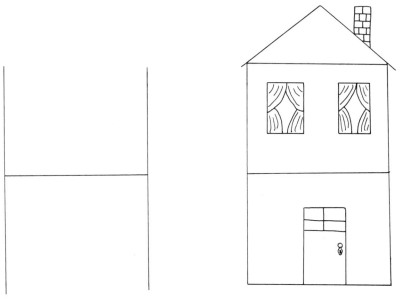

matches his he says, "Match," and that person must give him the card
If no one has a match they each turn over another card. The first chil
to find a match and say so, gets to take all the cards the other child ha
turned up. The game is over when one player is completely out of cards
The winner is the child who has the most cards.

37. To develop visual acuity, the teacher may draw a large face on the
chalkboard. Each child is given a chance to change or add one new
feature to the picture drawn. As each child takes his turn, focus attention
on one particular part of the total picture and on how the change
affected it. Children will need this discrimination later when letter
formation is introduced.

VARIATION: A scene or simple background drawing may be used.

Letter Formation

38. *Hint:* Many letters are frequently reversed and confused by children.
The teacher may point out that although many of these letters are
similar in shape, they face a different direction—for example, **b** and **d.**

Often a trick device may help children remember the difference in these letters. Children seldom confuse capital **B,** so this method may help them distinguish lowercase **b** and **d.** The lowercase **b** is just like the capital **B** without the top curve.

B   b

39. Instructional Aid. On sheets of oaktag (approximately 5"x15") write a letter of the alphabet in a bold manuscript. Cover this with an acetate sheet (or laminate). Child practices the form with a suitable marker. Directional arrows or numbers may be used to aid in proper formation. *Example:*

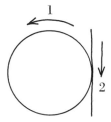

40. Instructional Aid. Cut letters from sandpaper or paint a mixture of Elmer's blue and sand over cutout letters. Students trace over a letter with their hands, then try to form it themselves. The rough texture aids in kinesthetic memory.

41. Pupils roll out modeling clay into long strings. They form letters by arranging the clay on top of large letters made by the teacher.

Word and Letter Discrimination

42. Lollipop Tree. A large tree is made from colored paper. In the green section of the tree cut small slits. Make lollipops by attaching colored circles to wooden sticks. On one side of the lollipops print letters of the alphabet. The children take turns picking lollipops from the tree. If they can name the letter on the back, they get to keep the lollipop. The child with the most lollipops wins.

43. Each child holds a letter and arranges himself in position to spell the word which the teacher writes on the board.

VARIATION: Alphabet cards may be used, and children arrange themselves in proper sequence.

44. Duplicated name cards are provided for a "Roll Call" game. Pupils match their desk name card with a card placed on the chalk rail. The children drop the copy from the chalk rail into a box labeled "We Are Here." They identify absent children by the names remaining on the rail.

Colors

45. The object of this game is to encourage the child to learn the color words. The child should put the correct colored egg into the correct nest.

blue   red   green   yellow

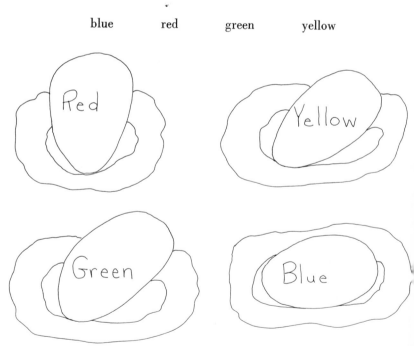

46. A large sheet of colored construction paper may be held up at the front of the room. Each child names an object visible in the room that is the same color as the paper. The game continues until all objects have been named.

47. Working with one color at a time, students collect pictures from magazines showing objects all the different shades of that color. (*Example:* blue.) Explain that the color is still blue but numerous shades exist. Mount the pictures for comparison. A partial color wheel can be added at the top of the chart to show the progression of shade change.

48. Using a colorful mail-order catalog, students locate and cut out items to be classified by color. These may be glued to color charts. For developing sentence structure, vocabulary and visual discrimination, they may play "I See" . . . (a red dress, or two red wagons).

IV. AUDITORY SKILLS

Rationale

The goal of discriminating auditorily among letter sounds and among words is founded upon many types of listening exercises. The child must first be able to discriminate pitch, loudness, duration of sounds and rhythmic patterns or sequences of sounds, for these are the auditory cues to letters and words. These auditory skills are also essential to phonic and structural analysis in order to discriminate among the pitches of letter sounds and of inflection, the loudness that determines accent, and the comparative duration of the sounds of vowels and consonants. Auditory memory functions in listening to words and syllable sequences.

Listening skills are also closely related to success in reading, for the thinking demanded parallels that used in reading. Listening is not a natural skill that matures with age; it must be trained. The goal of listening training is to facilitate the child's ability to do the types of thinking demanded in reading.

Children's ability to think in various ways in listening and reading situations depends directly upon the training given by teachers' questions. If questioning is limited to parrotlike recall of details, as is common in our classrooms, children will fail to develop skill in making judgments, inferences, conclusions, interpretations or evaluations. Listening training is an excellent opportunity to provide practice in these thinking skills, and thus to promote reading developments.

BEHAVIORAL OUTCOMES

The child will learn:

> to attend to and distinguish animal and environmental sounds
>
> to discriminate between loud and soft sounds
>
> to recognize pitch differences in common sounds and speech sounds
>
> to differentiate sounds of varying duration
>
> to respond to and remember the rhythm of speech sounds
>
> to recognize and remember sequences of sounds
>
> to follow directions
>
> to anticipate ideas in a context
>
> to retell or interpret continuous material
>
> to show comprehension of continuous material
>
> to show ability to form inferences, conclusions, judgments and evaluations of auditory material

Listening, Auditory Memory, Auditory Discrimination

49. Ask the children in a small group to close their eyes and be as quiet as possible for about thirty seconds. They will listen for sounds. When time is up ask a child to report as many sounds as he can remember (birds singing, feet shuffling or others).

50. For a mental exercise in auditory memory, the teacher pronounces unrelated words while the pupils listen: house, box, giraffe, chair, soup. Students recall named items as teacher asks:

an animal	piece of furniture
something to eat	a place to live

Difficulty and number of words used would depend on the maturity of the group.

51. Read a story or poem orally to the class. Have students listen for mental images and sound associations as you read. They may listen for colors, sounds, action words or descriptive words they pictured while they listened.

52. One member of a group of children is blindfolded, or covers his eyes, while another child hops, skips, runs, walks or gallops. The blindfolded child tries to tell from the vibrations what rhythm he hears or feels.

53. It is fun to tape voices and let members of the group listen and identify the voices they hear. Or, several children may go behind a screen. One child speaks. The group tries to identify the child's voice.

54. Auditory Rhythm in Action. Children are given cards marked with paths of squares. Give each child a marker of some sort. The teacher bounces a ball on the floor two or three times. Children move their markers according to the number of bounces they hear.

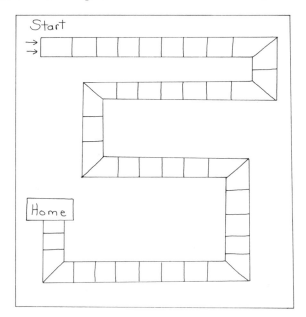

55. The group closes their eyes and listens while the teacher or another child does the following: 1) tears paper, 2) crumples paper, 3) bounces a ball, 4) taps table with pencil. Children try to discriminate what is being done.

56. *Hint:* As a dismissal technique, try this for auditory discrimination: "If your first (or last) name begins like 'Billy' you may go" (Betty, Butch or others). Continue with other initial sounds until all children are dismissed.

Chapter Three

BASIC READING SKILLS

I. LETTER AND WORD RECOGNITION

Rationale

The fundamental skill of word recognition is basic to all levels of reading. Unless the individual can recognize words and their meanings, reading is literally impossible. However, in contrast, letter knowledge is not significant for beginning reading. Word recognition is not aided by being able to name the letters of the alphabet, or even the letters within a word. To illustrate, word recognition involves attempting to say a word according to the sounds the letters represent, or the shape, or context of the word, and then, having pronounced it correctly, to recognize it mentally as a meaningful idea (word). The spelling of the word or naming of the letters does not initiate this recognition-meaning process. Thus, training in the names of letters is preparatory to writing and spelling, and preliminary to phonics, but irrelevant to the reading act. Only in highly phonic programs must letter names be taught as part of the process of learning to read, and then only to introduce letter sounds.

Some research has attempted to show that the knowledge of letter names is highly related to early reading success. The authors of these studies have ignored the patent fact that such learning is a reflection of the child's cultural background and the education of his parents. Economically-deprived children or those not of middle-class background do not know letter names before entering school, for obvious reasons. And no one is so naive as to attribute all the academic difficulties of these children to this oversimplified explanation that letter knowledge conditions success in beginning reading.

In keeping with current research on methods of beginning reading, letter names may be taught early, but primarily to permit the rapid introduction of writing, a potent reinforcer of beginning reading. Another argument for teaching letter names early is the marked trend toward the introduction of more phonics in the very beginning stages of reading. These are cogent reasons for teaching letters not dependent upon the meretricious argument that they enter into the act of word recognition.

One aspect of the process of word recognition that is often ignored is the difference between *meaning* words and *function* words. Nouns and verbs are meaning words with definite mental associations that help the child recognize them. If properly taught with pictorial or action associations, such words are relatively easy to learn. But words like prepositions and conjunctions are almost meaningless, and therefore usually quite difficult to recognize in isolation. Function words are learned by auditory language experiences with phrases and sentences, where they are used in correct, familiar language patterns. When the child is reading, he recognizes **to, by, in** or **for,** not because the word is really meaningful, but because the word would normally occur in the phrase or sentence, as he remembers hearing it many, many times. For these reasons, we do *not* suggest trying to teach lists of these function words, except in meaningful settings. Once nouns and verbs have been learned through pictures or actions, they can be practiced over again, without these reinforcing clues. But other types of words are not learned by practicing with them in lists. Only by pictures, or by use in actual phrases or sentences, do function words achieve some degree of meaning and learnability.

BEHAVIORAL OUTCOMES

The child will learn:

> to recognize his own name
>
> to recognize labels on common objects

to first match and later name letters in both capital and lower-case forms

to write letters correctly and consistently in manuscript

to match and compare word shapes

to match and later copy simple words such as nouns and verbs

to recognize simple words in sentences by their shape and/or context

Own Name, Numbers, Letters, Matching Letters, Capitals, Lowercase, Knowledge of the Alphabet

57. Make a large whale or fish out of poster paper or colored construction paper. On the whale print all the capital letters of the alphabet. Underneath, make twenty-six small fish and print one lowercase letter on each. Children match the capital and lowercase by attaching yarn from letter to letter. This may be done as a bulletin board, or on a smaller scale and enclosed in acetate. If this is done, the children may draw a line to connect the letters with a watercolor marker. To make checking easier, use assorted colors.

58. Make six lotto cards with thirty one-inch squares. Select six letters of the alphabet for each lotto card. Repeat each letter five times on the lotto card. Each card and its corresponding squares may be a different color. This helps keep each set together.

Show or call out a letter, and have the player place a matching letter on his card. The first player to completely cover his card wins.

VARIATION: Use capital letters on the card, and lowercase letters on the individual squares.

This game fits nicely in a hosiery or handkerchief box for shelving.

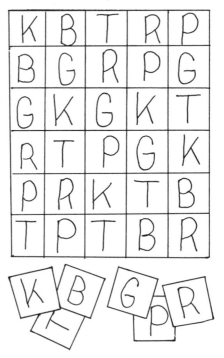

59. Give children sheets of paper with short rows of lowercase and capital letters printed on the page. They should make a ring around the capital letters or the lowercase letters.

AaaA   aaaa   AaAa   aaAA   Ddd   DDd   dDdd   dDDd

60. Oaktag or construction paper is cut into the longest strips possible. These strips should be five or six inches wide. The children measure off the appropriate size squares and fold them to make an accordion.

The sheets are taped together to form a twenty-six page accordion book. Each child may make his own book, or one large one may be made for the reading corner. Each page of the book is labeled with the appropriate letter. The child may either draw or cut out a picture to illustrate each letter or the sound it represents, and place it on the proper page.

61. Draw an elephant on the board and print letters of the alphabet all over him. Each child finds a given letter, reads it and then erases it. The object is to see who can wash the elephant clean. This game may be used for beginning instruction in alphabet recognition or for work on alphabetical order.

62. Divide a large sheet of paper or oilcloth into thirty squares. Write a different letter of the alphabet in each block and print stars in the four remaining blocks. Print several small cards for each letter of the alphabet. Standing ten feet away, each child tosses an eraser on the sheet. He receives a small letter to correspond with the one on which the eraser lands. He forms as many words as possible from the letters he collects. If the eraser lands in a box with a star the child may choose any letter he needs to make a word. The child with the most words at the end of the game is the winner.

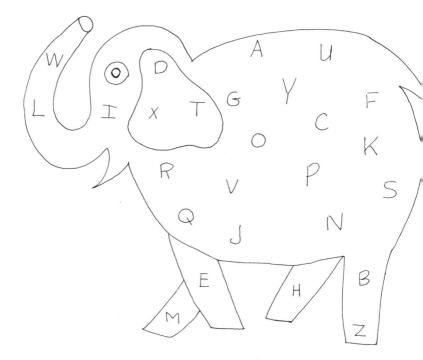

Word Configuration, Matching Words and Phrases, Compound Words, Word Recognition

63. To help children with words easily confused or reversed, use the "stop-and-go" method. Write these words on individual cards, printing a green dot under the first letter and a red dot under the last. Tell the children to observe the traffic light colors—start on green, and stop on red. The child is then given two cards: one with colored dots, one without. *For example:*

64. Several columns of words are printed on paper. A key word is printed at the top of each column and also appears somewhere in the column. Place a sheet of acetate over the paper. The child is asked to circle the key word as it appears in each column.

For example:

cat	door	was	saw
can	drop	went	(saw)
car	dune	(was)	say
(cat)	(door)	wash	see

65. List pairs of words with similar structure. Have students circle the parts in each word which are alike, and underline the parts which are different. This may be used effectively with the overhead projector.

1. (c_a_t) (c_o_t)

2. do(or) m(or)e

3. (gr_ow_) (gr_een_)

4. play(ing) look(ing)

66. Nonsense sentences may be used to point up the differences in similar words. Write one sentence containing both words. Read and discuss word differences. These sentences may also be used for practice with letters frequently confused. *Examples:*

> That *was* the duck I *saw.*
> The *children* gave the *chickens* their feed.
>   or
> The *boy* has a *dog.*

67. Write on chalkboard or transparency pairs of words easily confused through spelling reversals: **pan, nap; rat, tar; was, saw; draw, ward.** Use one word of each pair in a sentence and have students indicate the one you used. After noting the similarities in visual detail, discuss the differences in spelling and meaning. Then, have students make sentences using both words in each pair.

68. If a child confuses two similar words, the word causing the trouble is written on transparent paper. The child places the transparent paper over several sentences containing similar words, until he finds the word exactly coinciding with his problem word.

69. A set of thirty-two or more printed word cards is used. Each word should appear on four cards. The players are dealt five cards each and five are placed faceup on the table. The remaining cards are placed facedown. The first player checks to see if he can match any word he holds in his hand with one on the table. If so, he pronounces the word and places the pair in front of him. If he cannot pronounce the word, he places the matching card faceup on top of the duplicate and the next child has his turn. He follows the same procedure. The next player may match a word card on the table or a pair in front of a player. A player may keep the matching cards only when he holds all four of a kind. If a player is unable to make a match, he draws one card from the pack and discards one from his hand. The game continues until all the cards are played. The player with the most sets of cards wins.

70. Phrases from sections in the reader are written on cards and given to the children. The children then examine the sections and try to match the cards with the phrases in the reader.

71. A cardboard tube such as is used in the center of a carpet or linoleum is cut to about a five-foot length. Paint the tube green and cut slits along the side, into which flash cards may be inserted. Cut several leaf shapes from green construction or poster paper and print a sight word on each. Phonemes, prefixes or words for any skill needing practice may be used instead of sight words. Insert the leaves into the slits on the tube, to resemble a beanstalk. At the top place a box, simulating a castle. In the box place a small paper castle for each child. If the child correctly climbs the beanstalk, he gets his castle.

72. Each spot on the clown, or other figure, bears a word. The child tries to learn all the words on the clown.

VARIATION: Use detachable spots (plastic discs) ; the child puts them on the clown as he learns the words.

73. With chalk, divide a small section of the floor into blocks several inches square, or into spaces as on a ladder. Allow as many spaces as there are words in the game. Toy figures represent each player. Place the figures on the starting line. The leader holds up a word card. If the first child reads it correctly, he advances his figure one space. The game continues until one of the figures crosses the goal line.

74. This is an excellent way to have children practice problem words while having fun. An airfield is made by drawing a spiral path on a sheet of paper. A hangar is placed at one end. The field is divided into sections. One word is listed in each section. Each player has a duplicate set of word cards. The two players place their airplanes at the starting line and the game begins. The first player reads his top card. If he reads it correctly and it is the same as the first word on the runway, he moves his plane to that space. If not, he may not move and that card is placed on the bottom of his stack. The player may continue until he misses. The other player then takes his turn. The winner is the first person to reach the hangar. Additional runways may be made to clip on as new words are learned.

75. The teacher makes duplicate cards, using words causing configuration trouble or words needing practice. All cards are placed in an envelope. The child matches words which are exactly alike. This activity

may be used as individual practice or as a game, allowing one point for each pair made within a given time.

76. On the bulletin board tack three pictures of words to be rhymed; below each picture tack a manila envelope. On a table place a box containing words (printed on 3"x5" cards) that can rhyme with the pictures. Instruct each child to take a word card, read it to the group and place it in the envelope beneath the picture with which it rhymes.

Example:

pictures of:	Cat	Bell	Rake
word cards:	sat	tell	cake
	fat	sell	lake

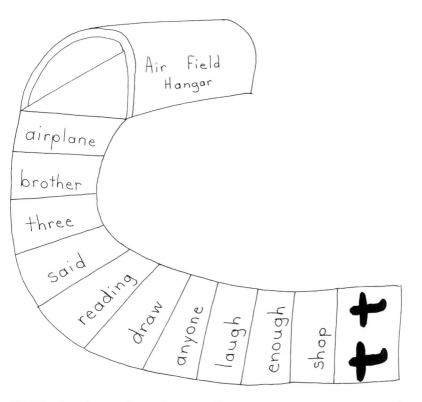

77. Word cards may be used to play dominoes. Variations may be used to match words, opposites, initial blends or rhyming words. Regular domino rules are used.

78. Stress the importance of consonants as the framework of most words, noting that one's familiarity with the details of a word enables him to visualize the entire word with only a glance. Write sentences in which all vowels are omitted and have students read them:

> Th_ w_nd _s bl_w_ng.
>
> Th_ b_rthd_y p_rty w_s f_n.
>
> Th_ h_rs_ j_mp_d _v_r th_ f_nc_.

FOLLOW-UP: Students may wish to write notes to friends in this fashion.

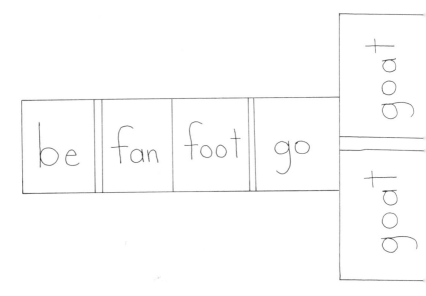

79. *Hint:* When stressing word recognition avoid continual use of rote learning techniques. Memorization of sight words is an ineffective teaching practice. Occasionally games and activities may be used calling for isolated sight words, but they should always involve a sense of fun.

80. List ten words with which children are having difficulty. If a child can read all ten words, he launches the rocket.

Can you launch this rocket? Start the "countdown" at "10."

81. "Target Practice." Can you hit a bull's-eye by making sentences using all the words on the arrows?

82. On a sheet of poster paper draw a football field divided into ten sections, with a goal line on either end. Begin by placing a small tag with each player's name on it on the fifty-yard line. Half the cards should face the opposite end. Direct the first player to read the word or answer the question which the teacher has prepared in advance. If he answers correctly, he moves his name card ten yards toward the opposite goal; if he fails, he moves his name card ten yards toward his own goal. When a child crosses the opposite goal line, he scores six points, then returns to the fifty-yard line.

83. Make a chart containing nine pockets, three on each row. One word card is placed in each pocket. Each player is given duplicate word

cards with spaces marked either **X** or **O**; these are kept in an envelope. One child is given the "**X**" cards, and one the "**O**" cards. Each child is given a turn to read a word. If he can correctly read and match his word with a word in the pocket, he places his "**X**" or "**O**" in the

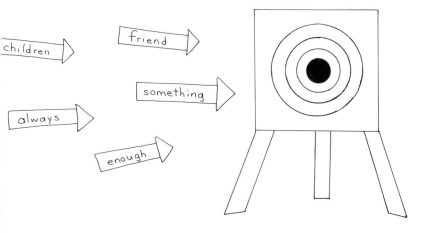

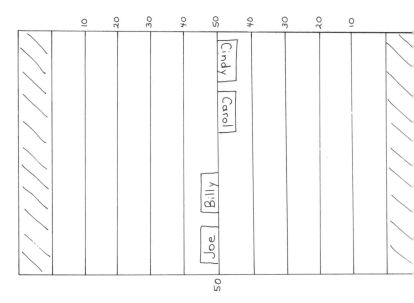

proper space. The rules are similar to regular Tic-Tac-Toe. The firs
one who has three across, three down or three diagonally across is th
winner. For variety, sounds, rhyming words or compound words ma
be used.

84. Each child is given a turn as phrase cards are flashed around th
group. If he reads the phrase correctly, he remains standing but if h
misses a card, he must stoop. If he correctly reads the following phras
card before the next child can respond, he rises and that child stoop
Any child correctly reading all cards is the winner.

85. Divide the outside edges of a rectangular board into squares. I
each square print different words and phonemes. Small squares c
numbered paper are kept in an envelope. These numbers will tell ho
many spaces the child is to move. He draws a card and moves hi
marker the number of spaces indicated. In order to stay on that spac
he reads the word printed on it; if it is a phoneme, he gives a wor
containing that sound. If he is wrong, he moves back until he lands o
a space containing a word he can read. Players take turns, and the gam
continues until a player reaches the finish line. Additional tracks can b
made using different words. These may be clipped on the board fc
variation.

Go back 4 spaces	monkey skip	spr	fish while	jump	talk
mother					whale wh
birds fry					trees in
tiger sh					candy cl
ticket yes					water plan
start ↑↑↑	bears cup	giraffe br	popcorn chin	sh scr	Miss a turn

86. Pairs of children play checkers as usual but they must read a word in order to move into another space. Words are printed in two directions, so that both players can read them. Vary the checkerboards to include compounds, one-syllable words, words using particular sound elements, social studies vocabulary, color words and others.

87. Make about thirty flashcards, on which are written words the class has studied. Be sure all the words are nouns which can be illustrated. Show the group each flashcard, and allow the children about two seconds to study the word. After all the cards have been shown, allow the group fifteen minutes to illustrate as many words as they can remember. Check by going over and reading the flashcards.

Sample list:

dog	bed	jacks	hand	lady
net	rag	map	log	truck

together	include	coverage	several
together	include	coverage	several
element	season	animal	weather
element	season	animal	weather
whose	syllable	check	elephant
whose	syllable	check	elephant
please	always	climate	desert
please	always	climate	desert

88. *Hint:* True compound words are not merely two separate words put together to form a new word. A compound word consists of two words, joined, to describe an object or expression in which *each word retains* its original meaning.

   Valid examples: **steamboat, housefly, railroad.**

   Invalid examples: **forget, into, before, understood, below.**

89. This activity draws attention to how compound words are formed. On 3″x5″ cards print compound words; then, cut between the two words which form the compound. Place the sections of ten compounds in an envelope and have the students fit the two parts of a compound together, making as many correct words as they can. Then, direct the students to write these words on a sheet of paper.

   Note: Compound words are valid only when each word retains its original meaning.

   Examples:

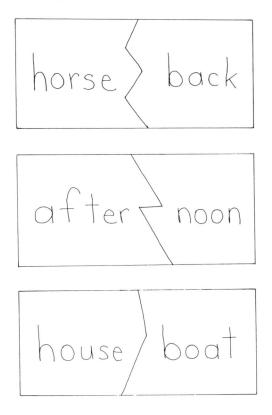

90. On the board draw a pair of pictures which will illustrate a compound word. Ask the students to say the names of each of the two pictures in the row, and listen for the new compound word. They join the two words together to spell the compound word.

cowboy

doorbell

playhouse

91. List phrases on the board and have students write a compound word for each.

Examples:

1. one who puts out fires   **Fireman**

2. side of the road   _____

3. time for bed   _____

II. CONCEPTS OF READING

Rationale

There are a number of concepts of using and interpreting books and pictures which are fundamental to the reading act. The most basic of these concepts of reading is the realization that *printed words are talking written down.* Other concepts are the directional flow of ideas in books and pictures, the sequential nature of stories and picture sequences and the permanence of the word arrangements in a poem, rhyme or story. Children should also learn to react to stories and pictures, to share their reactions in different ways with other children and to realize that books and pictures may suggest ideas and actions to the readers.

Physical handling of books and pictures, finding a story by its page number or other means and relating the pictures accompanying a story to the ideas offered in the text, are other important concepts of reading. These ideas must be understood by children if they are to use books and pictures intelligently and with pleasure.

BEHAVIORAL OUTCOMES

The child will learn:

that the words he or other children say can be written down (and later read)

to recognize the flow of ideas in a book—from top to bottom, from the beginning to the end, from left to right

to react to and interpret picture sequences

that a sentence says exactly the same things each time we read it

that we can enjoy stories

that we can share our recall of a story or picture sequence

that the pictures accompanying a story tell us something about the action

that we can do creative things to show our understanding and enjoyment of reading

Directional Orientation to Pictures and Books

92. To supply training in reading from left to right, the teacher gives the child paper ruled into blocks. The number of blocks will be determined by the number of letters in the words. Blocks are numbered from left to right. The child writes the words in the blocks. For example, if the word is **car,** the child writes **c** in the first block, **a** in the second block and **r** in the third.

This is a useful orientation exercise for crossword puzzles.

93. Using old magazines, the children find pictures of animals, cars, people or other objects facing left or right and paste them on charts labeled with the directional words.

94. Cut a simple cartoon strip such as Peanuts, Henry or Nancy into sections. Students arrange them in order as the events occurred. When selecting cartoons make sure the sequence is evident.

Action and Events Move Sequentially from Picture to Picture or Page to Page

95. A large book may be made by folding a piece of oaktag in half. Construction paper or drawing paper may be used for the pages. Bind the pages together with adhesive, or by stringing cord through holes punched in the sides. On the left pages of the book paste pictures either drawn by children or cut from old books. The right pages should have two slits cut wide enough to hold a sentence strip. Each child is given several sentence strips bearing a sentence to match one of the pictures in the book. The child goes through the book, placing the matching sentence strip beside the appropriate picture.

96. A short cartoon film or filmstrip is played without the sound. The children tell the story from observing the picture sequence.

97. Familiar stories may be written and cut up into sentences or phrases. The strips are mixed up, and all sentences for one story are placed in an envelope. Then, children try to arrange them in sequence to retell the story.

Telling, Interpreting and Relating Stories and Pictures

98. The teacher reads several lines of an unknown story to the children. They are asked to supply an ending. The story used may be an actual story to be read later or an original one started by the teacher. For example, the teacher reads, "Ted was a very sad little boy. All of his friends had pets of their own, but Ted didn't have a pet. One day, Daddy came home with a large box in his arms. Suddenly Ted heard a strange sound. He ran to his father and . . ."

99. Word and Picture Hunt. List words on the board that go with objects in a specific picture in the reader or other source. The children locate each corresponding object in that picture. This may be used as an oral lesson with a small group. The reverse may also be used as a written exercise. The children may be given pictures from magazines, books or other sources.

100. Ask a small group of children to bring a drawing to the circle. Let them tell a story about the picture. After each child has been given a turn, one or more stories may be selected to make up a group experience chart. After the children have started writing, spontaneous drawings may be used as a basis for writing as well as telling a story.

101. Project on the screen (using either an overhead or an opaque projector) a picture of people engaged in an activity. Encourage pupils to supply descriptions of the activity: what is taking place, who is participating and what they may be discussing.

FOLLOW-UP: Pupils may wish to compose a dialogue between the characters, either orally or in writing.

102. Project a picture on the screen (or have students study a picture in the text), directing the class to note the locations of objects and people. Then, remove the picture and encourage students to describe the place, relationships of the people or things with such words as "below," "next to" or "above."

103. For comparison, children may be shown several pictures including one that does not belong in the series. They are asked to find the one that does not belong. Loose pictures, comic books or strips may be used effectively.

104. Choose a story that dramatically narrates varying moods and emotions. Have students skim an assigned passage and identify which of the five senses are evoked, describing how the passage makes them feel. After every portion of the story has been examined, let the class capture the images and emotional tones through an oral reading of the story.

105. The class or group is divided into two or more teams. Each pupil is given an interesting magazine picture or diagram, a pencil and a piece of paper. Each child writes a sentence caption for his picture. If his caption is a sentence and if it expresses the main idea of the picture, he receives a point. The team with the most points is the winner. The object of the game is to help pupils learn to form a good summary sentence. For this reason, points are allowed only for complete sentences. Be sure to point out that phrases may also summarize ideas.

III. COMPOSING OWN STORIES AND EXPERIENCE CHARTS

Rationale

In the author's opinion, the most realistic approach to beginning reading is through the medium of experience charts. These are group or individual compositions on any subject of interest, written down first by the teacher and later, as they learn to write, by the children themselves. Unlike most readers, charts provide interesting, varied reading materials which resemble the language forms and structures already familiar to the children. The direct connection between reading and speaking is made obvious, for the children see the very words they have spoken written on paper. The chart approach makes realistic use of the pupils' auditory memories for speech and promotes the development of acquiring thoughts from printed words. A feeling for sentence structure and sequence is fostered, as well as the habit of reading from left to right. In contrast to the usual reader, the chart uses real language, familiar, concrete and spontaneous.

The chart approach equates reading progress with the child's verbal and thinking skills in a practical manner. Certainly no child can learn to read faster than his own experiences, and his auditory and speaking vocabularies, permit. This limitation is recognized most clearly in the experience chart usage, in contrast to all other methods of beginning reading. The reading materials that the child gradually learns to use are created out of his own language ability and experiential background. Every child learns to read the very words he knows best from his own life experiences. His reading ability grows in keeping with the development of his language and thinking skills, and his daily experiences—the only true way in which reading growth can occur.

BEHAVIORAL OUTCOMES

The child will learn:

>to participate in a group story composition
>
>to recognize the importance of sequence in a series of ideas or events
>
>to express his ideas in an organized manner
>
>to recognize various ways of expressing an idea
>
>to visualize ideas in printed form, to connect meaning with printed symbols
>
>to understand the concept of a sentence as a complete thought
>
>to express his own experiences in writing
>
>to read his own compositions and those of his classmates
>
>to use and understand simple punctuation (comma, period, question mark, exclamation mark)
>
>to read aloud with the usual inflections characteristic of speech

Dictated Stories

106. *Hint:* Experience stories may be compiled in the form of a book, or mounted on a hanger if they are written on large paper.

Fold the paper over the hanger, and staple or tape it at the top.

107. *Hint:* A child's first experience in dictating stories may be a simple statement such as, "That's me and my dog playing," when he is drawing a picture. The teacher merely writes his comment. Or, the child relates something that has occurred, such as: "Me and my Daddy went fishing yesterday." Write his comment without changing his grammar, and suggest he make a picture to go with his experience.

108. Early experiences in "writing" a story may be had through dictating it to the teacher. If he can, the child writes his own material. These stories may be written on large chart paper, or the teacher types the stories, using primer type, and binds them into a book. Children read their own stories or exchange them with other children.

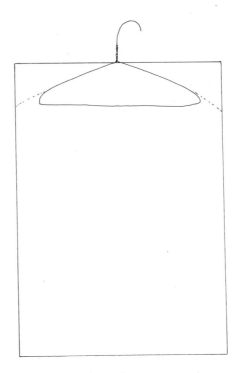

109. A small group of children shares interesting or exciting things that have happened to them. Let the group select one story as the most enjoyable. The group may then make up an experience chart based on the story.

110. Write an experience or class-created story on a chart or on the board. After it has been read aloud several times, go through it and erase parts of words (blends, digraphs, initial consonants or endings). Have several children read the story and "think out loud" the missing letters as they go. If you wish to stress one kind of sound, such as initial consonants, then erase the letters for only the beginning sounds. As an independent activity list the above examples on the board. Students should list the words from their story which fit or apply to the words written on the board.

111. Make a movie screen from a stiff piece of cardboard. In the center draw a rectangle 8"x12". At the top and bottom of the rectangle cut half-inch slits the length of the rectangle. The movie roll should be eleven and a half inches wide, to allow sufficient room for it to be pulled easily through the slits. The rectangle serves as the screen. Be sure phrases are spaced properly, so that only one story phrase appears on the screen at a time. Children will enjoy "reading" the movie phrase by phrase.

Creative Writing

112. Make a large "pencil" from a towel roll. Insert a cone shape for the point. A rubber chair tip serves as the eraser. Students make up story titles, and these are placed inside the pencil. As an independent activity, the student may select a title and write a creative story.

113. A good culminating activity for a postman unit is to have children exchange letters. After a discussion of letter form and sentence structure, the children are prepared to express their ideas in letters. Children draw names to make sure every child receives a letter. The completed letters may be mailed and delivered by a child selected as postman. The letters may also be read orally, calling attention to phrasing and punctuation.

114. Each child may make a booklet containing his own original stories. These may be about personal experiences, trips or just something that stimulated his imagination.

115. Purchase thirty animal picture postcards to encourage and motivate creative writing. Give each child one card, and have him write a story to go with the picture. Since each picture is different, the stories will also be individual. The same set of cards may be used several times during the year. Have the children write their names on the back of the card, so they will not be given the same picture again.

116. A unique way to display creative writing is to use a large picture frame (without the glass). Fold a piece of paper, the size of the frame, in half. On one half the children write or dictate a story; a crayon or painted illustration is made on the other half. Colored construction paper may be used for background mounting. Display a different story each day, giving every child an opportunity to share his story.

117. As an independent activity, students may write creative stories or make a picture scrapbook about themselves. A "Just Me" book may include information such as:

My family	What I want to be
My favorite things	My funniest dream
My best friend	My feelings about myself

The scrapbook may be made by stapling pages together or by folding strips into an accordion-type booklet. This same procedure may be used to show subject matter such as animals, Indian ways or machines at work.

118. Have the children write original stories about their family, neighborhood or community helpers. The stories can be presented to small groups by means of puppets, chalk talks, movies or the flannel board. If the flannel board is used, construction paper cutouts may be made and adapted for flannel board by gluing small pieces of sandpaper on the back. Children should also be encouraged to read fiction or fact books, and give book reports in the same or similar ways.

119. A small group of children compose a one-minute story. One child goes to the board and begins writing the story. He continues for one minute. At that time he must stop and call on another child. The next child continues the story from where the first one left off. Each child is allowed one minute to add to the story, and every child is given a turn. The last child writes a conclusion and reads the story to the class.

120. List words on the board that could be used to tell a story. Have the words read, and ask a student for an idea concerning a story which the words suggest. Call on several students for ideas. Each child begins writing a story, using as many of the words listed on the board as possible. At the end of two minutes each child passes his paper to the child on his right. That child will read what has been written and add to it. The papers are passed five times, allowing two minutes for each student to add to the story previously started. At the end the stories are read aloud and discussed.

Sample word list:

girl . . . frightened . . . storm . . . alone . . .

shadows . . . walk . . . path . . . dog

Chapter Four

WORD PERCEPTION

I. PHONICS

Rationale

For those children who possess the necessary auditory discrimination and vocabulary, phonics can be of real assistance in the beginning stages of reading. If the child can hear differences between letter sounds, and learn the common sounds that letters represent, he may employ these sounds in word recognition. With these basic learnings, he may blend the letter sounds into a facsimile of the word. If the word is then familiar auditorily, he may recognize it, and comprehend its significance in its setting. All this is really the process of phonic analysis.

Unfortunately, many teachers of phonics fail to appreciate the interdependence of this series of behaviors and skills which compose the apparently simple act of recognizing a word through phonic analysis. Many teachers stress only the learning of these sounds as though this were sufficient. They seem unconcerned about whether the child can really discriminate these sounds in reading, writing, speech and spelling (as well as in phonic exercises). They feel it is not important that some children do not readily think through words with the aid of auditory images; or that children of bilingual or limited background may not have any store of auditory memories for the words in the reader. Some teachers of phonics, as well as some authors of phonics systems, do not appear to realize that skill in blending sounds into recognizable wholes is an essential part of children's training. Finally, even many reading specialists ignore the fact that unless the blended word is quite familiar to the child, phonic analysis fails to produce word recognition. In common primary basal materials, the vocabulary is usually quite familiar; but in more difficult materials, as in content fields, unfamiliarity of the word or concept may render phonic analysis useless.

Because of these inescapable limitations in the actual usefulness of phonics, we recommend that it be taught only to pupils reading at primary levels. We assume that it is offered solely to those who have (or have learned) adequate auditory discrimination, auditory vocabulary and an aptitude for utilizing auditory cues to words.

Having taught readers the basic knowledge of letter sounds and blending, two problems remain in applying phonics to the act of reading. These are the usefulness of phonic principles and the task of conveying an habitual pattern of phonic attack. Recent research on phonic principles has revealed their applicability in common words taught in the first six grades. We have used this research to select a list of the most functional rules, e.g., those that apply to a reasonably large number of words and are true more than two-thirds of the time. To ensure the transfer of phonic learning into the reading act, one section is devoted to ways of teaching children a group of practical steps in using phonics to achieve word recognition.

Since phonics is a rudimentary word perception technique, it must eventually be replaced by more advanced skills such as syllabication. The introduction of common syllables in the phonic syllabus is, then, a necessary step in this developmental progression. As with phonic rules, these common syllables are carefully selected in terms of their stability and usefulness.

BEHAVIORAL OUTCOMES

The child will learn:

> to distinguish the common sounds of single letters (as they function in words, not merely as isolated sounds)
>
> to distinguish the sounds of consonant and vowel combinations

to recognize that some letters are silent in words

to blend letter sounds and combinations into word wholes

to recognize a number of common syllables as integrated units

to apply certain phonic principles

to develop a systematic approach to phonic analysis

PHONIC SYLLABUS

Our review of the Clymer, Emans and Bailey studies (see Spache and Spache, *Reading in the Elementary School*, second edition [Allyn and Bacon, Inc.], pp. 390–401) of the utility of phonic generalizations resulted in an abbreviated phonic syllabus, using those aids that seem dependable in pronouncing words.

At the preprimer level:

1. When the letter **c** is followed by **o** or **a,** the sound of **k** is likely to be heard.
2. When there is one **e** in a word that ends in a consonant, the **e** usually has a short sound.

At the primer level:

3. When **y** is the final letter in a word, it has a vowel sound.
4. When **o** and **a** are next to each other in a word (i.e., **boat**), the **o** is long and the **a** is silent.

At the first reader level:

5. When **c** is followed by **e** or **i,** the sound of **s** is likely to be heard.
6. When **c** and **h** are next to each other, they make only one sound.
7. **Ch** is usually pronounced as it is in **kitchen, catch** and **church,** not like **sh** (French pronunciations are sometimes borrowed, as in **Chevrolet**).
8. When two of the same consonants or vowels are side by side, only one is heard.

9. Words having double **e** usually use the long **e** sound.

10. The **r** gives the preceding vowel a sound that is neither long nor short.

We suggest that, for second grade and up, the teacher make a large wall chart, giving the student a guide to aid him in pronouncing an unfamiliar word. This guide can be of great assistance when students are reading independently. The chart should be in bold print, with key words written in contrasting bright colors for emphasis.

The steps should be discussed and reinforced continually with the students, so that they fully understand how the chart can aid them.

WHEN YOU MEET A NEW WORD

1. What is the sound of the first letter or blend?

2. Finish reading the sentence. What makes sense here with this beginning sound or blend?

3. How many vowels are there? Where are they?

4. If there is one vowel in the beginning or middle, try the short sound of the vowel.

5. If there is one vowel and **e** at the end, try the long sound.

6. If there is one vowel at the end, try the long sound.

7. If there are two vowels in the middle or at the end, try the long sound for the first vowel, except in **oi, oy, ou, ew** or **ui.**

8. Say the whole word. If this doesn't sound right, try the other vowel sound.

9. Now do you know the word? If not, write it down and get help later.

10. Go on with your reading!

Initial Consonants

121. As the roll is called, each student stands and points to an object in the room which has the same beginning sound as his name. *For example:* Mark may point to a map.

122. Mimeograph a large circle divided into eight sections. In the middle make a smaller circle, and in each section designate an initial consonant. Have the children illustrate one or more objects which begin with the letter given. Students may also write the word for the object they have drawn.

VARIATION: One consonant may be printed in the middle of the circle, and pupils draw or cut from magazines pictures which begin with the initial consonant.

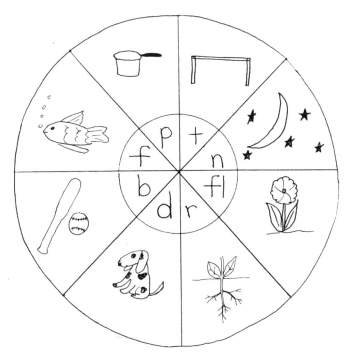

123. On a sheet of oaktag, draw two columns of pictures. Punch a hole next to each picture, and attach a shoe lace or yarn next to the pictures in the first column. For each picture in the first column, draw one in the second column which begins with the same sound. The children match the beginning sound by threading the shoe lace to the corresponding picture.

124. Two or four children may play this game. Cards (2″x3″) are made, each containing directions for moves. A folder is made showing a path. Pictures also appear in various places on the path. Place the

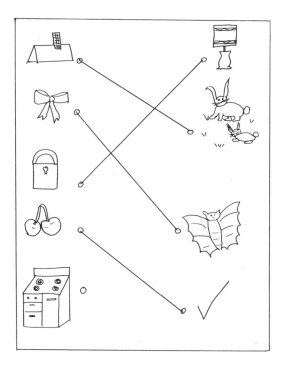

cards in the middle of the table, facedown. Each child draws a card and moves his button according to the directions. Directions may include blends, rhyming words or pictures to match initial sounds. If a child moves past a picture, he gives a rhyming word or another word beginning like the name of the picture he passes. If the card he draws indicates a picture he has passed, he moves five spaces back. If two players stop on the same space, the second one moves back ten spaces. The first one to reach home wins.

Directions for rhyming words or initial sounds cards:

1. Move to a picture that rhymes with "sat."
2. Move two spaces past something that rhymes with "cow."
3. Move to something that begins like "shoe."
4. Move to something that begins like "train."

125. Make an orange tree from colored poster paper or oaktag. Mount it on poster paper, and make several slits in the leafy part of the tree. Cut out small oranges from construction paper, and print a consonant

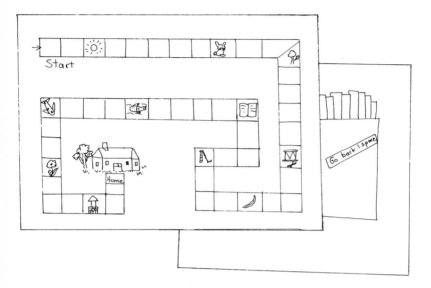

or blend on each one. Place the oranges in the slits. A small basket is made to accompany the tree. A child picks an orange and gives a word beginning with the sound printed on it. If correct, he places the orange in the basket. If wrong, the orange must stay on the tree. This may be used as a small group activity for free time or as a means of dismissing a child from a skill lesson.

126. In this game you use a shoebag with various consonants and blends printed on the front of the pockets. Picture cards are given to the players. They try to place their cards in the right pocket.

127. Small objects are placed in a box. Such things as a toy car, spool, pencil, crayon, paper clip or eraser may be used. The child draws an object from the box. He names the object and gives another word which begins with the same initial phoneme. The game continues until all the objects have been used.

128. Divide a 5″x8″ card into twenty-five squares, similar to a Bingo card. In each square print a consonant or blend. Give each of four students a card and slips of colored paper the size of the squares. Gather pictures whose beginning sounds correspond to those printed on the Bingo card. To play the game, hold up a picture (of a finger, for example). If a player has **f** on his card he will cover it with a slip of

paper. When a player has five spaces in a row covered either vertically, horizontally or diagonally, he is the winner.

129. Complete the words below by supplying the first letter or letters. Students compare their list with a friend's list, to see how they differ and to ascertain if they are valid words. They should come up with as many new words as possible.

___ay	___ight
___ump	___at
___ing	___ate

130. Independent practice with similar sounds may be used in picture word drills. Cut out small pictures of objects beginning with two similar sounds, such as **f** and **v** (small pictures from primary workbooks are excellent for this). Place the pictures in labeled envelopes. Children empty the envelopes and sort the pictures according to the two sounds. When this is completed correctly, they sign the envelopes to show they

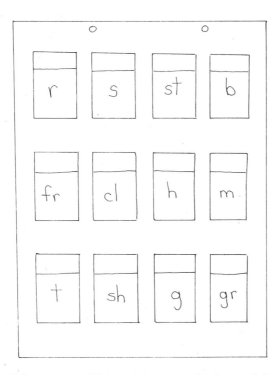

have finished the exercise. This activity may also be used for compound words, blends, opposites, rhyming words or vowel sounds.

131. Divide oaktag into ten equal sections, 3″x1″. Print one word in each section. Use words that contain initial consonants and phonograms being studied. Cut the words into two equal parts, dividing them after the initial consonant. Place all the pieces in an envelope and have the children assemble the words. Several combinations may occur, such as:

c - at   c - an

f - an   f - at

132. A small group pretends they are going on a trip. Each child in the group names an object he will take beginning with the letter **B**, then each names an object that begins with **C.** Continue naming objects for one letter until someone misses or fails to think of a new word beginning with that sound. In that case, go on to the next consonant in the alphabet.

sn	r	n	th	d
t	st	c	w	cr
ch	b	s	tr	p
fl	m	br	g	sl
r	sh	dr	cl	f

Example: **"B"**—Children may name things such as **balloon, ball, barrette** or **bacon.**

133. A set of twenty cards, 2″ square, may be made by the teacher or students. On each card print a different consonant (omit **y**). Each child in the group must have an entire set of twenty cards. Have each child place his cards in rows across his desk alphabetically. The teacher pronounces a word, and each child holds up his card that shows the beginning sound of that word. The teacher may use a word list similar to the following for each game. Be sure the list contains words beginning with each letter.

Example:

goat	wasted
kit	house
daughter	money
someone	peanut

This exercise may also be done with vowels.

134. "I Spy" may be played with small groups of children to review initial consonant sounds. Each child takes his turn spying an object which begins with a particular initial sound. For example, he might say, "I spy something that starts with **t**." They may guess things such as **toy, tape, television** or **table.** The person who guesses correctly is "it."

135. Many children have difficulty relating to pictures of things. It is easier for them to learn initial sounds by seeing and holding objects which begin with that sound. Shoe boxes may be labeled with a designated initial consonant sound. Inside, place some small objects which begin with the sound printed on the box.

For example:

> **b**—ball, balloon, book, bottle, bow
>
> **c**—cork, candle, comb, cup, coconut
>
> **d**—dish, doll, daisy

136. Ask children to draw a scene of their choice. Have them look at each object in the picture and say its name to themselves. They determine the beginning letter of the object, and write that first letter on top of the object in their picture. Label as many objects with the letters that say their correct beginning sounds as possible.

VARIATION: Children draw a picture, making sure that each object in the picture begins with a given letter (such as "**C**"). A group game may be created by drawing a picture on the board; one child at a time comes to the board and labels an object in the picture. He says the name of the object, gives the beginning sound and writes the letter that makes that sound.

137. Cut twenty-five 4" squares of oaktag. On five cards, write five initial sounds being studied in class. On the remaining cards, illustrate four pictures of objects which begin with the same sounds as each lettered card. Paste scraps of flannel or sandpaper on the back of each card so it may be used on the flannel board. During activity time, let a child place the letter cards in a row on the flannel board. He then matches the pictures with the beginning sounds by placing them beside the correct letters. Students take turns acting as "checkers" to see if they are placed correctly, thus giving further skill reinforcement.

138. Mark off several squares on wrapping paper or oil cloth. Each square bears an initial consonant. A permanent marker or colored mending tape may be used for marking the oil cloth. A child throws a beanbag into the squares and names as many words as possible that begin with the consonant sound printed in the square where the bag lands. One point is given for each word named within a set length of time. This exercise may also be used with rhyming words.

139. Often remedial students have trouble learning initial consonants. Try making vocabulary lists for special interest areas. The student or group of students may take each consonant in alphabetical order and list related words for a given subject. The teacher's own knowledge of her children's special interests is very helpful, of course.

For example:

Cooking:

b—bake

c—cantaloupe

d—dishtowel

f—fish

g—ginger

Other examples for girls' interests:

Dolls, pets, art, clothes

Examples for boys' interests:

Football, fishing, baseball, cars

Special holidays:

Christmas, Easter, Thanksgiving, Hallowe'en, Valentine's Day

140. Divide a piece of tagboard, 9"x9", into nine squares. In each square draw a picture containing the letter or letters for a sound being studied. Print part of the word under the picture and omit the sound being stressed. Make small cards showing the letter or letters which have been omitted. The small cards are kept in an envelope and clipped to the tagboard. The child looks at the first picture and says the name of the object to himself. He finds the missing part of the name by looking at the small cards in the envelope. He completes the word by adding the card to the initial sound, and goes on to the next picture.

VARIATION: Use only pictures in each square. The small envelope will still contain the sounds used in the pictures. The child looks at each picture, then finds the sound it contains. Answer sheets may be included for self-correction.

141a. After working on the **qu** sound, list several sentences on the board. Omit the **qu** word in each sentence. Have students read the sentences and fill in the missing **qu** word.

Example:

> The king's wife is called a _____. (queen)
>
> Do not be noisy, please be very _____. (quiet)
>
> A twenty-five cent piece is a _____. (quarter)

141b. A small group may also play a "show me" game with this same sound. Give each player one large card, blank on one side and the letters **qu** on the other. Read a list of words to them. If they hear a word with the **qu** sound, they are to hold up the card showing the letters **qu.** If the word does not contain the **qu** sound, they hold up the blank side. Word lists may include: **quickly, talk, quote, question, card, goats.**

142. Each child in the group is given a letter of the alphabet. When he is called on, he gives the name of a bird, beast or fish beginning with the sound of the letter he holds. The caller may ask the child to classify the word he gives, stating whether it is a bird, beast or fish. Limit initial sounds to those you want to stress.

143. Instructional Aid. Label small boxes with initial, ending or medial consonants. Words or letters needed for various activities could be drawn from the boxes when needed. Words with prefixes, suffixes or other elements may be used also.

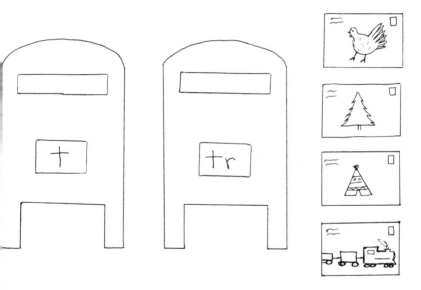

144. This travel game develops awareness of the initial sounds of words. One student may say, "I am going to drive my automobile to *Canada.* Will you help me plan the trip?" Students will help by answering the following questions, using only words with the initial sound of **c** as in Canada.

> What kind of car shall I drive? (convertible) (Chevrolet is **not** a possible answer)
>
> Who will accompany me? (Carol)
>
> How will the weather be? (cloudy)

What large city will we travel through? (Carrollton)
Where may we stop for lunch? (cafeteria)
What shall we eat for lunch? (carrots)
Where shall we stay in Canada? (cabin)
When should we return? (Christmas)

When all questions have been correctly answered, the student w
answered the last question will then begin a different trip, using qu
tions devised by the teacher in advance. If more than two questio
concerning the first trip are incorrectly answered, the driver must beg
again.

Blends and Consonant Digraphs

145. Making digraph booklets can supply useful reinforcement f
phonic information. Pictures of objects beginning with digraphs, su
as **ch, sh** or **th,** are cut from magazines. Use a separate booklet for ea
digraph. Have students glue in the pictures and print the word for ea
object under the appropriate picture.

146. Give the turkey his tail feathers by writing in as many words as possible that begin with letters printed on the feathers. This is an excellent exercise during the Thanksgiving season.

147. A mat is made from a piece of oilcloth 1½ yards square. Divide it into sixteen blocks. In each block, print one of four blends and digraphs with a permanent magic marker.

A spinner is made, using a square divided into four sections labeled "left foot," "right hand," "left hand," "right foot." The four blends are printed in each section.

Make a separate word card for each blend. On each word card, list several words containing that blend.

One child spins, to find the section and blend on which the spinner lands. He then selects a word from the appropriate word card and says it. The other two children find the blend and place the appropriate hand or foot in the proper square. The game continues until one child loses his balance and falls or gives an incorrect response. Only three children may play at a time.

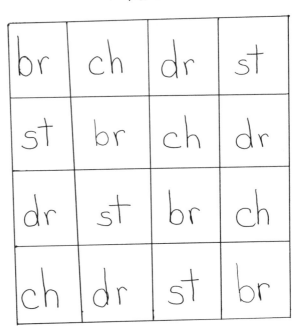

Mat

148. Students divide a piece of drawing paper into sixteen square
Colored paper should be cut into one-inch squares for markers. Mak
enough markers for each child to have sixteen. On a chart or on th
board, list foundation-letter combinations, such as the ones show
below. Have students print one letter combination in each block, but n
in the same order as the ones on the board. The teacher pronounces
word containing a blend or digraph and one of the sounds given. T
child finds the sound on his card and puts a marker on it. When a ro
of letters is complete, either across or down, the child calls out "Lucky
If he has marked the correct squares, he is the "Lucky" winner and
new game begins.

Examples of letter combinations:

(**ch**) op		it
(**sh**) ut		ip
(**st**) ab		an

Spinner

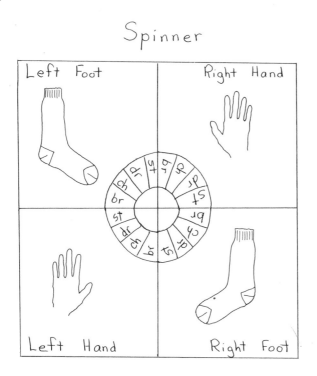

| Left Foot | Right Hand |
| Left Hand | Right Foot |

149. A large clock may be made from tagboard or poster paper. Attach a tagboard hand in the center with a brad, so it will turn freely. Around the outside edges of the clock, print some blends or digraphs. Let a small group of children work with the clock. Each child will be given a turn to spin the hand and give a word beginning or ending with the sound on which the pointer lands.

150. Divide the class into four relay lines (teams). Write four beginning blends or digraphs on the board and have the lines stand in front of the four sets of letters. When the signal is given to begin, the first person in each line writes one word using the initial blend for his line. After writing the word, he gives the chalk to the next person on his team and returns to his seat. The race continues until one line is completely seated; if the team has used their starting blend correctly, they are the winners.

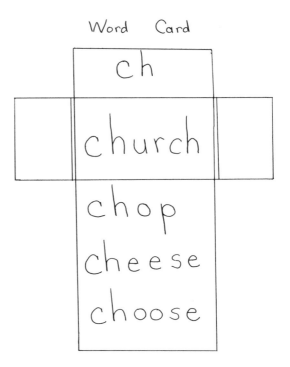

Word   Card

ch

church

chop

cheese

choose

Example:

WH	FL	CR	GR
white	fly	crow	green
whistle	flop	cry	grow
why	flutter	cross	grass

151. The teacher reads several words beginning with the same in blend. The children listen to the beginning sound. Then, tell them letters that represent this sound. They supply other words they k that begin with that blend. After several blends are learned, they be placed in a small box. Children draw cards and give words begin with that blend.

152. A ladder or other object may be drawn on the board. On rung, write a blend or digraph. Let a child go to the board and "c

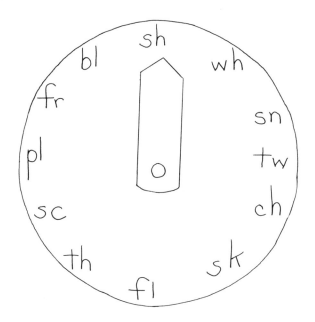

the ladder" by saying a word that begins with the blend or digraph listed.

VARIATIONS: Use a sliding board or a train, with sounds coming out of the smoke stack.

153. After a word element has been studied, give the children old books or magazines. They then look for the word element in the printed material and circle any words containing the sound. For example, if the element is **ch,** the child would circle such words as **chop, church** or **match.** Each child checks a partner's work.

154. Make twenty slits in a large piece of oaktag, so that cards 3″x4″ can be inserted by paper clips. Print a word or sound on ten of the cards, with a duplicate card for each one. On the back, number the cards from one to ten (make two of each number). Place the cards on the board, with the words or letters facing the children. The group is divided into two equal teams. The first child comes up to the front, and must say the word or sound and find its mate before he turns the card over to see if the numbers match. If they do match, they remain with the numbers showing and his team is given one point. If they do not match, the cards are turned back so that the words or sounds are

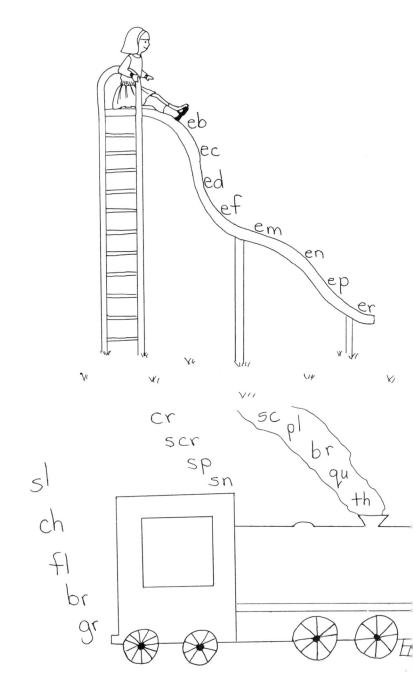

eb
ec
ed
ef
em
en
ep
er

cr
scr
sp
sn

sc
pl
br
qu
th

sl
ch
fl
br
gr

86

showing. A member of the opposing team is given a chance to match two numbers by calling out and turning two other cards. The game continues until all cards have been matched, and the team with the most points wins the game.

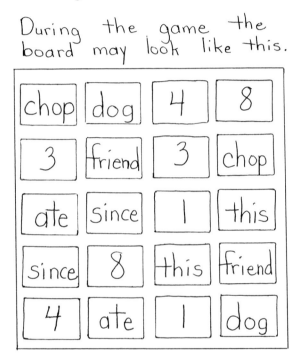

During the game the board may look like this.

chop	dog	4	8
3	friend	3	chop
ate	since	1	this
since	8	this	friend
4	ate	1	dog

155. For use in small groups, prepare one-word flash cards using such words as:

tr	ch	st
train	chicken	stay
truck	child	story
trick	chin	stick
true	church	store

Give each child two cards. Instruct the players to listen carefully as the teacher pronounces a word whose initial sound is the same as one

of the groups of cards. For example, the teacher says the word **stati**
each player who has a word beginning with the **st** sound will stand
his place, show his card and pronounce the word distinctly.

Short and Long Vowels

156. "Simon Says" can be played to check students' knowledge
sounds, endings, syllables or other language skills. The teacher
make a statement. If the information is true, the players will put t
thumbs up; if it is false, they will put their thumbs down. If a child g
an incorrect response, he is out until the next game. The last per
remaining in the game is the winner.

> *Sample statements:*
> 1. Simon says, "short **a** says $\overline{\text{a}}$." (thumbs down)
> 2. Simon says, "long **e** as in **beat**." (thumbs up)

157. Divide the group into teams of no more than four members ea
Each team is given a sheet of words with the vowels missing. Memb
work together to list as many different words as possible using differ
vowels.

> *Examples:*
>
> | _t | t_p (e) | cl_p | m_k_ | r_g |
> |---|---|---|---|---|

When the time limit is up, the teams exchange papers to check valid
The dictionary may be used for verification of correct words.

158. Draw five pictures across the top of a transparency. Be sure e
picture contains a different long vowel sound. Number each pict
from one to five. Divide the lower part of the page into three colun
List several words containing long vowel sounds. After each wo
draw a blank. Have a child come up and find the picture at the top
the page which has the same vowel sound as the word in the colu
He is to write the number of that picture next to the word. (This e
cise may also be done using short vowel sounds.)

159. Write on the chalkboard these words: **rattle, fiddle, gobl
fable** and **circle**. Have students pronounce each word and iden
the vowel sound in the first syllable as either long, short or **r**-contro

use	_5_	grow __	came __
why	_3_	cube __	ride __
boat	_4_	lake __	acorn __
cake	_1_	float __	feet __
she	_2_	by __	game __
leaf	_2_	bee __	beat __

Remind the class that the consonant before the **le** begins the last syllable, then ask them which letter begins the second syllable in each of the listed words.

160. A fun game to play for sounds review is "Guess the Object." Objects which contain the sounds being reviewed are placed in a small sack, one item per bag. The bags are then stapled shut, numbered and labeled with the sound studied. By using the senses of touch, hearing, smell and sound, the students try to identify the object in each bag. Their responses are written down as each sack is passed around the room. After all the sacks have been passed around and checked, a child may open each sack and check the responses for correctness and spelling. (A cloth sack with drawstrings may be reused for years.)

Example: Long vowels—each bag may contain one of these:
   boat   rope   pine needle   tape   bone   light bulb   cube

161. After several different vowels are introduced with short sounds, practice should be given in context reading. The children may be given a sentence containing a blank, and three words to fill the blank. Each multiple-choice word has a different medial sound. They are to circle the correct word to complete the context of the sentence.

For example: She wrote with a ____ (pan, pen, pin).

162. Divide a sheet of paper or transparency into squares. In each square, draw an object which contains either the long or short sound of the same vowel. Under the picture, write the name of the object and beside the name leave a blank for the answer. Ask the child to label the picture "long" or "short," depending upon the vowel sound contained in the word.

163. A sheet of paper or transparency may be divided into squares. In each square, illustrate an object containing a long or short vowel sound. A blank should be provided for the response. Ask the child to look at the picture and indicate the vowel sound heard in the word by filling the letter in the blank. The sheet may be covered with acetate or laminated, for repeated use.

164. A list of words may be written on the board. The words should contain long, short or silent vowel sounds. Have the students write the words and mark the vowel sounds in each word.

Example:

1. cāke̸

2. we̲

3. gōa̸t

4. cŭp

5. u̲se̸

6. ŭp

165. After the class has studied vowels, several sentences may be written on the board. Ask the pupils to be good "detectives" and find the number of vowels contained in each sentence. A blank should be provided at the end of each sentence for their response.

VARIATION: The children may write a note to a friend. The friend must count the vowels in the note, and return it with the correct answer. Use children's names often in the sentences.

Examples:

1. Alice picked a bouquet of flowers for her mother. __17__
2. Bob went to the store with Sam. __8__

Blending Sounds into Words

166. Half the class receives cards bearing consonant sounds; the other half, word families (such as **ill, all, at**). The children holding consonant cards pass through the class to find their partner and make a word. As partners are found they tell the word made by combining their cards. Continue until the entire class is paired.

167. Two circles are cut from oaktag, one larger than the other. On the larger circle, print final sounds; on the smaller circle, print the beginning part of a word. Fasten the two circles together with a brad. The pupil makes words by matching the beginning and final sounds. He writes the valid words, which are then checked by a partner.

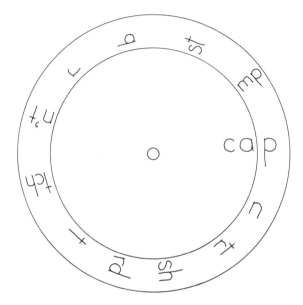

168. Cut two poster board strips, 2″x5″. On one strip, write an initial consonant or blend; after it, cut two horizontal slits 2¼″ long. On the second strip of poster board, write endings which will blend with the initial sound to form words. By sliding the second strip through the horizontal slits in the first strip, children can combine the two parts to form words.

VARIATION: Put a root word on one strip and an ending on the other. Use this exercise with small groups, so that blending skills can be checked.

169. Five squares are drawn on the blackboard. A consonant is placed in the left-hand corner of each square, and several phonograms are listed. A child is asked to give the consonant sound and then blend it with the phonograms to make words.

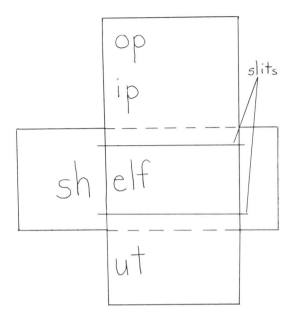

170. The teacher draws three circles on the board. In the first circle, she puts consonants; in the second, vowels; and in the third, consonants. The child makes a word by using a letter from each circle to form the beginning, middle and final sound of his word.

171. Cut a dozen or more one-inch squares from wood. On each side of every block, print a different letter of the alphabet. A permanent felt tip marker may be used. Vowels and common consonants should be duplicated often. Then, cut the top from a large plastic bleach bottle to use as a container for the wooden blocks. Each child takes his turn and spills the blocks from the container. Without turning any blocks over, he makes as many words as he can with the letters showing. A point is allowed for each word formed. Time may be kept by using a one-minute egg timer.

172. A large figure may be made from construction paper and placed on the board for display. On different parts of the figure, print syllables that can be matched into words. Have a child name a syllable sound and find its matching part, to make a word.

173. A sheet of paper is divided into fifty or sixty blocks, and a letter is printed in each one. Exercises are duplicated for the children. They

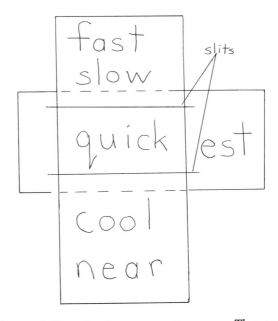

try to make words by going from square to square. They may move up, down, diagonally or across.

Example: By moving from square to square in any direction, find as many words as you can that tell things you could see at a farm. Possible answers are: **egg, lamb, chick, milk** and **pony.**

174. Cut small squares from oaktag and make several for each letter of the alphabet. Blends and digraphs may also be printed on the cards. Sort these according to beginning letters, and keep them in separate compartments of a box. The small cups of an egg carton are excellent for this purpose. Let children practice forming words by taking the necessary letters from the carton and laying them out on a table or desk. Stress making words they know or have heard before, and have them build the words from memory.

Silent Letters

175. Two students spin the center arrow. When it stops, the player moves the **e** marker (which is attached underneath the arrow) to that position. He must give sentences using the word with both the long and

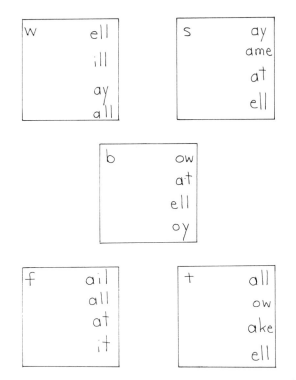

short vowel sounds. Score may be kept. Additional discs may be placed over the card, for variation of word patterns.

176. Have students list words that end with **ight.** (Be sure they remember that **gh** is silent in **ight.**) Have them make sentences with the words.

177. Flash cards may be made from oaktag. On the front of each card, write a base word or a word that can be changed by adding the letter **E.** On the back of the card, write an ending or the letter **E.** When the card is folded, the ending should touch the base word. Let the children practice making new words by adding endings or changing the word, with the addition of the "magical **E.**"

178. Instructional Aid. On inexpensive window shades, write lists of one-syllable words containing short vowel sounds. Opposite each word, write the same word again, but add the silent **e** that gives the word a long vowel sound. Shades roll up for easy storage.

Caution: This principle is valid less than half the time, so choose your words carefully.

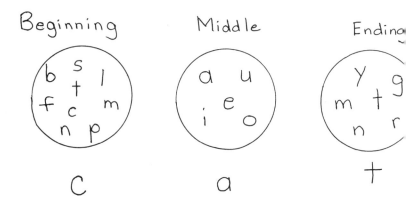

Vowel Digraphs and Diphthongs

179. A variety of objects are placed on a table; the names of the objects should contain sounds which are being studied in class. Divide the class into two teams. One child comes to the table and listens for the sound called. He is allowed thirty seconds to find an object on the table the name of which contains that sound. He picks up the object, repeat the sound and names the object. The teacher writes the word on the board and underlines the appropriate letters. If the player is correct he takes the object to his seat and a person from the other team comes to the table. After all the objects have been selected, the game is over The team with the most objects is the winner.

> *Examples of sounds and objects:*
>
> **ai**—(mail)   **ēa**—(beads)
>
> **oy**—(toy)   **ōw**—(bow)

180. Phonetic index cards may be used to relate vowel sounds directly to objects. Children may bring in various objects (or pictures) such as nails, raisins, thread or needles. The objects may then be attached to a 3″x5″ index card, using tape or glue. The teacher helps print the word names of the objects, omitting the vowel digraphs or diphthongs they contain. Cards are placed in a cigar box, recipe box or other suitable container. Children draw a card from the box and name the object shown on the card; then, on a separate sheet of paper, they write the

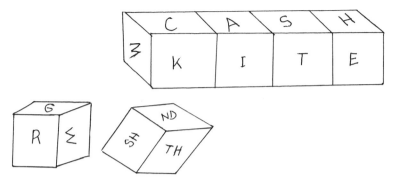

word, filling in the omitted digraph or diphthong. If facilities permit, the entire card can be laminated, permitting the children to mark directly on the blanks. Or, small pieces of acetate can be glued over the word.

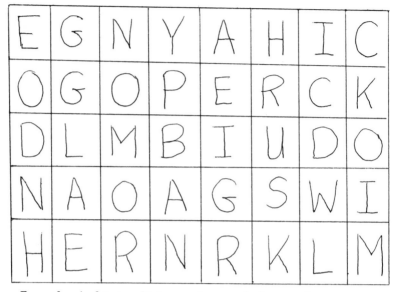

Example of objects which may be attached to cards:

boat	**b___t**
needle	**n___dle**
seed	**s___d**
handkerchief	**handkerch___f**
raisin	**r___sin**
thread	**thr___d**
nail	**n___l**

181. Write a **oo** word for each meaning. Children will add to the list from their independent reading.

Examples:

Middle of the day	_____	**noon**
One who prepares food	_____	**cook**
Not warm	_____	
Part of a plant	_____	
In a short time	_____	

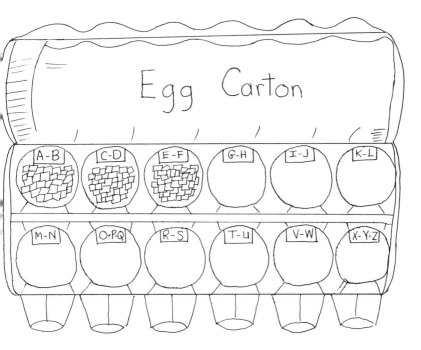

182. Mimeograph a sheet showing three kites, with adequate space beside each. On each kite, write a word containing a diphthong. Students may write sentences using words which rhyme with the words on the kites or which contain the same diphthong.

Controlled **R**

183a. *Hint:* The sound of **r** is not presented as a single sound when it occurs in the middle or at the end of the word because it follows a vowel and is modified by it:

as in fl<u>oo</u>r: **score, tore, more, four**

as in p<u>oo</u>r: **sure, cure, moor**

as in h<u>ea</u>r: **fear, steer, clear, peer**

as in h<u>ear</u>d: **bird, shirt, word, hurt**

as in th<u>ere</u>: **share, bare, fair, pair**

as in st<u>art</u>: **cart, guard, garden, heart**

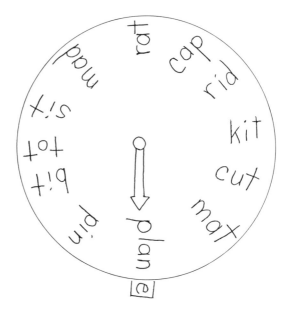

183b. Place the following combinations on the board or as headings at the top of a page:

er   ere   ar   are   or   ear   ir   ur   ore

Instruct the children to find words that fit the pronunciation pattern of the **r**-controlled vowels (*not necessarily the spelling patterns*), for each heading above.

Three- and Four-Letter Phonograms

184. Instruct students to listen for words that rhyme with a given word. Read a series of words that rhyme and one or more that do not rhyme. When they hear nonrhyming words, they clap their hands.

Example: The teacher says, "Listen for words rhyming with **pig** and clap on nonrhyming words—**big, fig, run, dig, hop.**" The children should clap on the words **run** and **hop.**

185. The teacher thinks of a word, then gives clues so the children may try to guess the word. Use this activity for concept development and rhyming word practice.

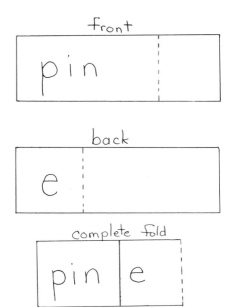

Example:

 a. I am thinking of a word that rhymes with **hen.** A pig lives in one.

 b. My word rhymes with **hair.** You sit in it.

 c. I am thinking of a word that rhymes with **plant.** It is small and lives underground.

 d. It rhymes with **train.** It falls from the sky. Plants need it to grow.

Other words:

ball—fall	**dog**—frog	**jump**—stump
boot—toot	**dish**—wish	**mop**—hop

186. To help learn names at the first of the year, make up simple rhymes using children's first names. Use these when you call the roll. Later, rhymes may be made with the last names.

Examples:

 Bill climbed up the hill.

 Fred stayed in bed.

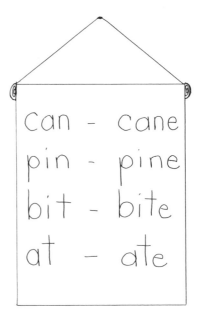

187. A game of catch may be turned into a rhyming word exercise. One child throws a ball and says a word. The child who catches the ball must say a word that rhymes with the one given. This may also be used for initial sounds.

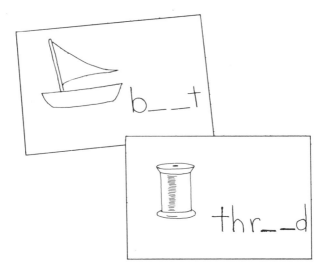

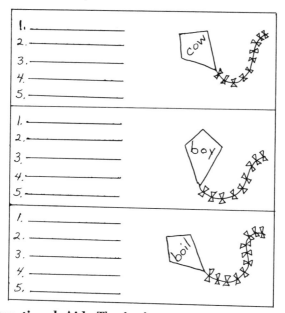

188. Instructional Aid. The bookworm is excellent for displaying rhyming words. Each hump bears a word that rhymes with words printed on other humps. The device below is mainly for display areas such as bulletin boards.

189. The children are divided into four even teams. Each team captain is given a large card with a family ending printed on it. Each team has a different word family. At the opposite end of the room, word cards are placed in the chalk tray. The cards are placed so the words may not be seen. Be sure you have as many word cards for each family as there are team members. At a given signal the children race to find a word card belonging to their family. The first team to have every member holding a card bearing a word belonging to their word family wins.

Examples:

pill	**play**
still	stay
Jill	Ray

190. Make a list of several words on the board. Have students write as many rhyming words as they can for each.

> *Examples:* (words need not conform to spelling patterns)
> 1. **can**—fan, ran, man, pan, ban, Nan, tan, van, plan (swan, not acceptable)
> 2. **dog**—
> 3. **clay**—day, prey, sleigh
> 4. **and**—

191. Place along the chalk tray a number of flash cards, on which have been pasted pictures of rhyming objects; e.g., a picture of a cat and a picture of a hat. Have a child go to the board, pick up the first card and name the object. Then, direct him to move along the board until he finds a picture which rhymes with that on his first card. If he selects a rhyming picture and pronounces both words correctly, he keeps the cards.

192. Small Group Activity. One child is selected as "police captain" and the other children are "policemen." The teacher tells the captain she is "Mrs. Ate" and has lost her children. The captain tells the police to hunt for the missing "Ate" children. Some check the "Bureau of Missing Persons," which is a box containing many words, some belonging to the "Ate" family. Others look in the park (on the counter), etc., where other cards are placed. The policeman locating the most children receives a "promotion" and becomes police captain.

193. Word cards or pictures of items that may be obtained at a particular store are prepared. One person distributes several cards to each player. The leader says, "Who has bought something that rhymes with the word **hurt**?" The player who holds a card that rhymes, reads it and then puts it into a bag at the front of the room. For example, if you were using a clothing store, someone may have a word or picture card for **skirt** or **shirt.**

VARIATION: Divide the room into two teams, and choose a scorekeeper. The participants may keep the cards, since they may be used for several responses.

194. Divide a sheet of paper into several blocks. In each block, illustrate two rhyming words. Label one of the pictures in each block. Have students label both drawings by changing the initial sound. The sheet may be done as a ditto or placed in acetate for repeated use.

195. A list of word parts may be made on a chart and left at the front of the room. In free time, the students practice writing as many words as they can which contain the sounds listed. Possible words may be listed on the back of the chart for self-checking.

Examples:

1. **at**—cat, sat, rat, fat, mat, bat, pat, hat
2. **ell**—bell, tell, fell, well, shell, dell, sell, cell

196. Have the children make up jingles to illustrate word families. A booklet may be made from the jingles.

Examples:

A **boy,**	A **cat**	An old **witch,**
Named **Roy,**	And a **rat,**	etc.
etc.	etc.	

197. A schoolhouse is made from stiff paper or oaktag. Several windows are cut out and a strip is glued to form a pocket for the "family" name. The school is labeled with a "family" name or word family previously studied, such as **ell** or **ame.** The child is given several small cards each containing one consonant sound. These cards should be small enough to fit into the windows of the school. Roll is taken to find how many "children" are present today. The "children" are known words that can be made by putting an appropriate consonant in the window to form a word with the "word family."

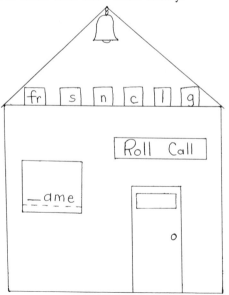

198. On 3″x5″ cards, print words such as these, one word to a card:

hill	fat	hall	free	fight
still	sat	ball	see	sight
fill	bat	fall	he	height
bill	hat	stall	bee	bite

Also print four cards with the word "transfer." Deal five cards to each player. Instruct the first child to lay down a card and name the word; have the next player lay down a card that rhymes or begins with the same letter.

Example: If the first player laid down **hill,** the second might play **still** or **hat.** When a player cannot play from the cards in his hand, he draws from the deck until he can play, or until he has drawn three cards. If he has a "transfer" card he may use that card for any word in his hand. The first player to get rid of all his cards wins the game.

199. Balls are cut out of oaktag or cardboard and decorated to represent a baseball, football or other object. A phonogram or ending is written on each ball. Two slits are cut so that a strip of paper containing initial consonants may be pulled through. The child makes a new word by substituting different initial consonants.

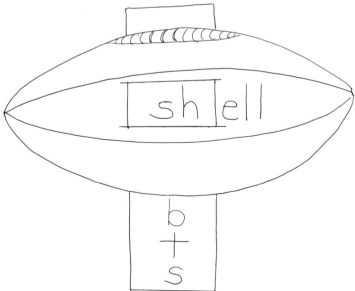

200. A transparency for the overhead projector may be made to review sounds. Illustrations picturing objects which contain the sounds being reviewed are drawn. In each square, under the picture, write the word of the object, omitting the letters which give the sounds being stressed. Have a child come to the overhead and complete the word by filling in the missing letter or letters. This may be done by omitting initial consonants, blends, digraphs or by giving the initial sound and omitting phonograms.

201. In each answer to the following clues, you hear the word **at.** This is a fun way to review rhyming words or three- and four-letter phonograms.

> *Example:*
>
> > A disagreement is called a __**at**.
> > A domestic animal that chases mice is a _**at**.
> > You wear it on your head. _**at**
> > *Answers:* **spat, cat, hat**

202. Several cards are made with words containing different vowel sounds. Cards should be shuffled and four given to each player. A small pack is left facedown on the table. The first player reads one of his cards. If another player has a card that rhymes, he must give his card to the caller. The pair makes a book and is placed in front of the player. If a player fails to get a rhyming card from another player, he may draw one card from the pack on the table. If he doesn't draw a rhyming word or if he can't read the card chosen, he must discard the card he called. The player with the most books wins.

Final Consonants

203. Read a word orally. Ask the children to give another word or find an object in the room, that has the same final sound.

204. To develop awareness of beginning and ending sounds, this game is played by two children. The teacher first pastes on cardboard eight small pictures of such objects as: sled, coat, boy, dog, rug, jar, desk and cup. Print on sixteen 3″x5″ cards the beginning and ending letters

Initial Consonants

_agon	_all	_ et
_oon	_at	_op
_ouse	_ook	_un

ack, ick, uck, ock

cl _	s _ s	j _ s
t _	st _ s	d _
bl _	p _	d _

of the picture cards, with only one letter on a card: for example, **s** and **d** for "sled." Shuffle the cards and deal each player eight cards, facedown. Place the picture cards in the center of the table and have both players sit facing them. Each player in turn takes the top card of his pile and places it to the left of the correct picture if the card is a beginning sound; to the right, if it is an ending sound. The player who places the second card next to the picture takes it, the winner being the player with the most pictures.

205. Divide the class into two teams, in lines facing each other. The first player on one team pronounces a word, such as **want,** and uses it in a sentence. The first player on the opposing team then says a word which begins with the *ending* sound of the previous word (e.g., **team**), and uses it in a sentence. The next player will use a word beginning with an **m** sound—and so on, in progression. A child who fails to make a correct response adds a point to his team's score. The team with the *lesser* number of points is the winner. Caution children to use words which begin like the other word *sounds*, not like it is *spelled*. If one child uses the word **cake,** the opposing player should omit the silent **e** and use a word beginning with a **k** sound.

206. To develop awareness of the position of letter sounds in words, have students draw three columns on their papers. As the teacher says a word, the students will draw a circle around the column which represents the position of the letter sound designated by the teacher or write the symbols in the correct column.

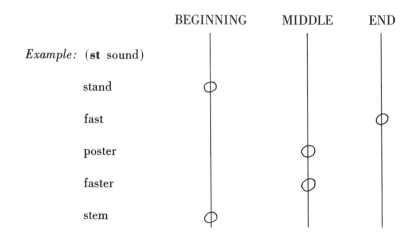

II. STRUCTURAL ANALYSIS

Rationale

Another fundamental approach to word recognition is through structural analysis. This involves reacting to words in terms of their inflectional endings, internal changes in sound and spelling, and simple prefixes and suffixes. Such analysis also demands the recognition that two words may be telescoped into one, as in contractions, or added together to form a compound word. It does not include the attempt to recognize small words within larger ones. This technique fails because of the variations in pronunciation of common words appearing to function as syllables. The influence of accent, or the loudness of syllables within a word, is a minor facet of structural analysis. Finally, there are a few principles of structural analysis for which the research indicates some practical usefulness.

BEHAVIORAL OUTCOMES

The child will learn:

> to recognize the effect of inflectional endings upon word meaning
>
> to recognize the effect of simple prefixes and suffixes upon word meaning
>
> to be familiar with internal changes in words in spelling and pronunciation
>
> to use accent as an aid to correct pronunciation
>
> to recognize common contractions
>
> to apply certain structural principles
>
> to recognize compound words

Contractions

207. Write several sentences on the board. In each sentence, underline the two words needed to form a contraction. Students substitute the correct contraction for the two given words.

Example:

He will go to the party with you.

He'll

I am sorry you are sick.

I'm   you're

208. After working with the contracted form of **not,** the following exercise may be used. Help children give contractions in which **not** is shortened. The following list may appear on the board:

will not	would not	were not
is not	had not	has not
should not	have not	does not
can not	was not	
did not	could not	

209. Write a one-paragraph story calling for many contractions. Students fill in the blanks with the missing contractions.

Example:

I _____ feeling very well. My throat hurts, so I _____ talk very loudly. I _____ take my medicine, so Mom said she _____ let me talk on the phone. I sure _____ do that again. Maybe _____ be better tomorrow.

Capable students may enjoy making up similar stories.

Plurals

210. *Hint:* In order for children to use plurals correctly when they need them in creative writing, make a colorful chart with the following information:

MAKING PLURALS

1. Regular nouns add **s.** (caps)
2. Nouns ending in **s, ch, sh** or **x** add **es.** (dishes, boxes)
3. Nouns ending in **y** preceded by a vowel add **s.** (days)
4. Nouns ending in **y** preceded by a consonant change to **ies.** (babies)
5. Nouns ending in **f** or **fe** usually change to **ves.** (calves)
6. Some nouns become different words. (mouse, mice; man, men)
7. Some nouns do not change. (sheep, deer)
8. Some nouns change some of the time. (fish, fishes—all of one kind, fish; several kinds together, fishes)

211. Divide the class into two teams. Say slowly, but only once, three nouns, such as **house, toy, girl.** Then, direct the first player on one team to say the plurals of these words in the sequence in which the teacher said them. Teams will alternate answering until every child has had a turn.

One point is given to a team for each correct plural given in the directed sequence. The team with the most points is the winner. After the first round is over, begin the second by naming three nouns whose plurals are irregularly formed: **mouse, half, leaf** and so on.

212. Write on the chalkboard a list of words whose plurals are variously formed. The class says or writes the correct plural for each word and gives the correct spelling.

shelf	moose	woman
potato	baby	donkey

Word Structure

213. The awareness of little words within larger words that *aid* in the pronunciation of the larger words can be helpful. This type of activity may be used effectively with the overhead projector. The child may underline or circle the little word or words he is able to see and *hear* within another word.

For example:

(can)dy, (cow)boy

(*not applicable:* some, father)

214. To develop students' ability to infer definitions of derivatives of obvious root words, write pairs of sentences on the chalkboard to be read aloud. Students identify the derivative and discuss how its meaning has been altered in relation to the root word.

> He spends much time in **study.**
> He is a **studious** boy.

> She will **receive** the prize.
> She was the **recipient** of the prize.

> It will **please** me to go to the party.
> It was a **pleasant** party.

Accent

215. List sentences on the board or on a ditto sheet. Use homographs (words with identical spelling, different meanings and sometimes different pronunciations) in each. By studying the context, students can determine the pronunciation and place the *accent* mark in the correct place.

Examples: Mark the accent to show correct pronunciation:

1. Father was **present** to **present** the gift.
2. The farmers were not able to **produce** enough **produce** for the market.
3. The author was **content** with the **content** of his article.
4. If you do not **address** the letter correctly, it may not be delivered to the right **address.**
5. The manager will **object** to this **object** being in the office.

The dictionary may be used to check pronunciations.

216. Upper grade students will benefit from making their own sentences using homographs. The sentences should clearly indicate which pronunciation is correct. The dictionary will be in constant use during this activity.

wind	live	excuse	convict
conduct	annex	subject	close
refuse	rebel	contract	protest
lead	read	produce	permit
perfect	object	combine	content

Roots, Prefixes, Suffixes

217. Instructional Aid. A chart or ditto may be made, asking for comparison in size or degree. After each question, draw three varied objects. Such questions as: "Which is the smallest?" "Which is the brightest?" or "Which is the largest?" may be used. This activity is best used in a small discussion group.

218. Have students divide their paper into four large squares. In each square, write three comparative adjectives and have students illustrate each one.

For example:

tall	short	cold
taller	shorter	colder
tallest	shortest	coldest

219. Four cards are made for each base (root) word to be studied. On each card, write the word four times, adding **ed, s, ing** or other elements to the base word. Each time, place a different word form at the top as the key word.

For example, the four cards for **work** would be:

work	**worked**	**works**	**working**
working	works	work	worked
worked	work	working	works
works	working	worked	work

Make cards for several different base words.

Directions: Each player receives six cards. Place the remaining cards in the center. The players group all cards with the same base word. When a player holds four cards for the same base word, he makes a book and places it in front of him. He then calls out one of the three words below the key word. If another player has a card with that word on it, he must give it to the caller. He continues calling until he fails to get a card from the pack in the center, and discards. The person with the most books is the winner.

220. Root words with endings may be listed on the board or shown on the overhead projector. Students may take turns marking the root word and circling the ending.

Examples:

1. walking	4. greatest
2. quickly	5. teacher
3. calls	6. balanced

221. List several words on the board. Then, ask which words can be changed by adding **s.** The ending is added in colored chalk. Continue using as many endings as possible. If the same word can take several endings, it is rewritten each time, using the new ending.

Examples:

play	happy	smile
got	run	and

222. Write several sentences on cards, omitting an appropriate ending. The child has an envelope containing various endings. His job is to select the appropriate ending to complete each unfinished word.

For example:

> June is walk____ to the store.

VARIATION: Use a variety of forms within the sentence. Have the child circle the correct one.

> My toy is (new, newer, newest) than your toy.

223. The teacher may prepare several paragraphs, omitting several word endings. The child is asked to supply the endings.

> Tom and Jim were outside play___ ball. They had two ball___
> Tom threw the ball to Jim. Jim tip___ it with the bat.
> The next pitch was knock___ into right field. They play___ to
> gether all afternoon.

Use a transparency for self-checking.

224. Children make new words by adding **er** and **est** to each root word. They use each new word in a sentence. Additional practice should be given by using these words in their written work.

Example:

new   _____   _____

quiet   _____   _____

225. A letter or syllable added to the end of a word can change the meaning of the word. The suffixes **er** and **or** mean one who does some thing. Give each child a duplicated list of words, similar to the following, whose meanings are changed by the addition of **er** or **or.** The student writes the proper word for each item. This activity may be done orally with a small group.

1. one who visits	6. one who plays
2. one who teaches	7. one who seeks
3. one who leads	8. one who directs
4. one who hunts	9. one who instructs
5. one who flies	10. one who drives

226. Write base words on the board. The child makes new words by adding given suffixes. He tells the meaning as each suffix is added. Suffixes such as **ly, able, er, est, less** and **ness** may be used.

227. After class discussion, a chart is made showing suffixes and pre fixes learned. Many words may change meanings when a prefix or suffix is added. List these words on small slips of paper. Instruct each child to draw a specified number of slips. Using suffixes and prefixes, the child makes as many words as possible, bringing his list to be discussed the following day. This is a meaningful outside assignment.

Example: **pair**

paired,   despair,   repair,   impairment

228. Children are given a list of words for which to make opposite meanings by adding prefixes.

Example: add **un** to these:

lock   hitch   kind

Words requiring different prefixes to change the meaning may be listed together. Prefixes such as **dis, ir** or **il** may be needed. Sentences may be done orally or written, to show comprehension.

229. The children are given duplicated sentences and asked to mark out the words that do not belong in them.

Examples:

1. It is (safe, unsafe) to cross the street without looking.
2. The man was (kind, unkind) to feed the lost puppy.

230. List several new words on the board. The child analyzes the prefixes and suffixes and writes sentences to show the meanings of the words.

careful   unchained

precede   degrade

231. Several suffixes are listed at the left of the blackboard, and base words listed at the right. The child constructs new words by adding suffixes to suitable base words.

Examples:

ly   encourage

ment   care

ful   near

less   use

232. After studying prefixes, their meanings and usage, use the follow
ing exercise. List several prefixes on the board. Opposite them, list words
to which these prefixes may be added. A child goes to the board and
chooses one prefix. He draws a line from it to a word with which it may
be used. He pronounces the word and uses it in a sentence. This may
be done as a game by dividing the class into teams. In that case, a
correct response would earn a point for the team.

VARIATION: Use suffixes instead of prefixes, following the same
procedure.

233. Divide the class into two teams and assign each team a special
section at the chalkboard. Write a prefix on the board; e.g., **mis, dis**
or **re.** Instruct the first member of one team to take his place at the
board and write a word that begins with the designated prefix. For
example, if the teacher had written **mis,** the child might write **mislead.**

The first member of the other team then takes his turn, and the teams
alternate writing words. When one player cannot think of a word, the
other team gets an extra turn. When neither team can think of a word,
a new prefix should be used.

The team with the most words wins the game.

234. Discuss with the class the changing of a word's meaning by
putting a syllable (prefix) in front of the word. Then, give each student
a duplicated copy of words whose meanings become opposite when a
prefix is added.

Change the meanings of these words by adding one of the following
prefixes:

un	**im**	**dis**	**in**

Use each new word in a meaningful sentence:

1. polite	5. correct	9. accurate
2. safe	6. sure	10. convenient
3. possible	7. continue	11. certain
4. patient	8. clean	12. willing

235. On 3″x5″ cards, print root words whose meanings can be changed by the addition of a prefix or a suffix. Place the cards in a box. On the chalkboard, write several prefixes and/or suffixes, horizontally, to serve as separate divisions.

Divide the class into two teams. Direct the first child on one team to draw a root word from the box and make a new word from it by adding a prefix or suffix. He should place his card on the chalk rail under the corresponding prefix or suffix, pronounce the new word and use it in a sentence.

The teams alternate making words, with one point awarded for each correct word and sentence usage.

236. On 3″x5″ cards, print derivative words, such as: **untrue, thoughtless, greenish, friendly, action.** On the reverse side, print the root words. Place the pile of cards in the center of a table, with the derivative words faceup. Instruct the first player to take a card, read the derived word and name the root word. If he is correct, he keeps the card; if he fails to name the root word, the card is returned to the bottom of the pile.

The next player takes a turn, and the game ends when all the cards are used. The player with the most cards is the winner.

237. Write the base word for each of these words in an interesting sentence.

Example: elves—The **elf** was a funny little guy.

cries	forgiving
unhappy	disbelief
funniest	balloons
dresses	teacher

238. Bingo type games may be used for practice in many areas. They may be used with initial sounds, blends or with prefixes and suffixes. For the prefix-suffix game, write root words across the top of the card, and in the squares below, write prefixes, suffixes or both. When a word is called, the player looks down the root word column to find the prefix or suffix needed. If the word contains both a prefix and a suffix, his space must contain both in order for him to claim the word. He then places a disk in that square. Regular bingo rules are followed.

For more advanced students, mix the endings and omit the root words from the card.

Prefix - Suffix Bingo

pay	spell	lock	joy	please
re	mis	ing	en	dis
ing	re	un	ful ly	ing
pre	mis ed	re	ful	dis ing
ment	ing	un ed	en ment	ing ly

III. SYLLABICATION

Rationale

The basic purpose of syllabication is to enable the reader to pronounce the parts of a word and thus, hopefully, to recognize the word. Actually, many rules of syllabication commonly taught are really aids in dividing a word at the end of a line, and have little to do with aiding in pronunciation. For example, the principle that double consonants are usually divided into the two adjoining syllables, as in **but-ter,** is simply a writing convention and has nothing to do with pronunciation. Moreover, like phonic rules, the principles of syllabication vary greatly in their validity, in the proportion of times they actually apply. Some are always true, but others function in less than half the words in which we might expect them to do so. We have tried to confine our exercises to the application of the most useful principles of syllabication.

BEHAVIORAL OUTCOMES

The child will learn:

to recognize and pronounce common syllables

to apply a few basic syllabication principles

to divide words into syllables, pronounce the separate parts and blend them into a whole word

to use syllabication systematically as an aid to pronunciation

SYLLABICATION SYLLABUS

We do not believe in the memorization of these various syllabication principles. The concepts involved should be derived inductively from lessons planned to help pupils observe those concepts. The generalizations derived from these lessons should be kept as few and as simple as possible. Only those generalizations which clearly help in pronouncing a word should be emphasized. The purpose of this training is to gain a few basic concepts of how words may be divided into syllables in an attempt to pronounce them—*not* to produce perfect syllabication. In keeping with this reasoning, we suggest the following principles:

1. Every syllable has the sound of a vowel in it.
2. When the first vowel sound is followed by **th, ch** or **sh,** these combinations are not divided and may go with the first or second syllable (for example, **ma-chine, moth-er**).
3. When the first vowel sound in a word is followed by two consonants, the first syllable usually ends with the first of these consonants (for example, **bul-let, pic-ture**).
4. When the first vowel sound is followed by a single consonant, that consonant usually begins the second syllable (for example, **sta-tion, la-dies, ta-ble**).
5. In most two-syllable words, the first syllable is accented (for example, **hap-py, pen-cil**).
6. When a prefix is added to a root word, the root word is usually accented (for example, **in-side, dis-co-lor**).
7. If **a, in, re, ex, de** or **be** is the first syllable in a word, it is usually accented (for example, **a-ble, in-ter-est, re-**

cent, dé-cent, beí-ter). However, when these same syllables are prefixes they are *not* accented (for example, **be-sidé,
re-claim, in-viś-i-ble, pre-scribé**).

Our third syllabication principle implies that the vowel usually has
a short sound. The fourth principle implies that the open syllable usually
has a long vowel sound.

Division of Syllables

239. With a small group, the teacher pronounces a word. The children
hold up a small numbered card which tells how many parts are in that
word.

Example: If the word **cowboy** were called, the children would hold
up the card showing the number two.

After children have become familiar with small words, they may
enjoy figuring out the number of syllables in such words as **rhi-no-
cer-os** or **u-ku-le-le**.

240. If you use flash cards from a basal series, the students in the
group could each be given a small stack of two- and three-syllable words.
Placing their cards on the table, they divide the syllables with colored
strips of paper. Discussion should follow, with students talking about
their two-syllable and three-syllable words.

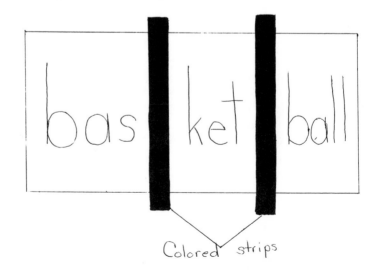

241. Divide a piece of paper into squares. In each square, draw an object whose name is spelled phonetically. The pupils sound the word phonetically and write it by syllables under the picture.

242. On the chalkboard, write a one-syllable word, a two-syllable word and a three-syllable word. On the chalk rail, place an envelope beneath each word. On a table, place a box containing word cards of one-, two- and three-syllable words. The student takes a word card from the box, reads it to the group and places it in the correct envelope, according to the number of syllables it contains.

243. On 3"x6" flash cards, list some vocabulary words. On the back of each card, write the number of syllables in that word. Keep the set together with a rubber band or in an envelope. This activity is best done by two players. One child holds up a card, with the word facing his partner. The partner reads the word, then tells how many syllables it contains. He then turns the card over to see if his answer is correct.

244. A syllabication exercise is made by printing multisyllabic words on the left side of an 8"x11" sheet of poster paper. Draw lines to the right of each word, so the student may write them by syllables. The correct responses should be written on the back, for self-checking. The poster paper can be covered with acetate for repeated use. Illustrations may be added, to make the cards more attractive.

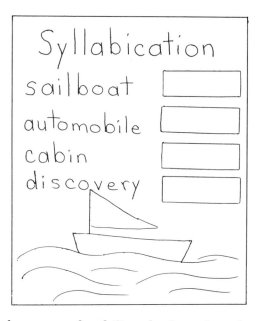

245. Make about twenty-five drill cards. On each card, print a word. Have students scatter the cards on a table and sort them according to the number of syllables.

246. Students who need extra help in structural analysis may arrange lists of words in columns, according to the number of syllables in the words. Words may fall into categories according to the interests of the students. Boys especially need interest-centered activities.

Example: ecology words

1	2	3	4
soil	water	erosion	conservation

IV. CONTEXTUAL ANALYSIS

Rationale

Readers of all ages constantly and unconsciously use the sense of the context to figure out the meanings of unknown words. Even primary children can read words in sentences which they can't recognize in a list, showing their natural use of the sense of a sentence in word recognition. Contextual clues are numerous, such as the position of the word in a sentence, figures of speech, actual definitions or explanations of a word, appositive phrases or clauses and the like. But we do not try to teach pupils to look for these structures in a sentence, in the way we teach them to recognize the relationships of the parts of a sentence. In reading, the child uses the contextual clues by thinking out the relationships, by drawing on his background of experiences with language through listening, speaking and reading. In other words, he responds to such clues as tone, mood and synonyms, not because he knows the terms to describe these things, but because he has experienced such sentences before and can sense, guess or feel the meaning. Hence, the goal of our exercises in contextual analysis is to promote thinking about the probable meanings of unfamiliar words, not to convey formal knowledge of their structural characteristics. Any of these exercises will be improved by having children discuss their thinking during the exercise, after they have completed it.

BEHAVIORAL OUTCOMES

The child will learn:

> to read an entire sentence before analyzing it for the meaning of an unknown word
>
> to react actively to possible clues within a sentence
>
> to show increasing skill in deriving word meanings from the context
> to combine the contextual clues with other clues, such as phonic, structural or syllabication
>
> to derive the pronunciation of a word from contextual clues

Idea Clues—Pictures, Experience (Inference), Comparison and Contrast

247. Children are given sentences using word pairs. One of the words is omitted in each of them. Beside the sentences, the omitted words are listed in mixed order. The child places a number before each omitted word to indicate the sentence in which that word belongs.

1. She had bacon and ____ for breakfast.   socks
2. Tom put on his shoes and ____.   coat
3. Put on your hat and ____.   eggs

248. A riddle book may be made up, with each page containing a new clue to the surprise object. As each new page is added, the child tries to solve the riddle. A picture of the object may be on the last page, or the object may be hidden in a package or a surprise box.

Example:

Page 1: I am small.   Page 3: I am small.

Page 2: I am small.   I am brown.

I am brown.   I live in a tree.

Page 4: I am small.

I am brown.

I live in a tree.

I eat nuts and acorns.

I am a ____.

249. The students are given sentences containing incompleted words. Using the context of the sentences, they try to write the words in the blanks by filling in the missing letters.

Examples:

1. The c____s were dark and it looked like rain.
2. Mother picked some f____s from her garden.

A continuous paragraph or story may also be used in this same manner.

It was a bright s____y day and Mark was getting ready to go on a t____p.

Their family was going to the m____s to visit some relatives.

250. *Hint:* Introduce a new word by giving a sentence that tells its meaning. Another method is to ask a question that will lead to the meaning.

Example:

> When your throat tickles you _____.
>
> What sound do you make when your nose tickles?

251. Children write brief stories substituting pictures for omitted words. This activity may also be done by writing stories omitting only the initial consonants. Children complete the words by looking at picture clues drawn above the incomplete words.

Example:

> Two little _oys went for a walk in the _oods. As they walked
>
> down the _ath, one _oy stopped. He bent down to look at
>
> a _orm crawling along the _ath. The other _oy heard a noise
>
> and looked to see a _ird flying from a __ee.

252. A short story using many familiar words of *similar appearance* is written on a chart, the board or ditto sheet. The story is read and discussed until the child clearly understands it. He is then asked to locate similar words and list them. After the listing has been completed, the child rereads the context to determine the difference in meanings of the words.

For example, the teacher writes:

> Troy has a toy tom-tom. Mom bought it for him.
>
> A new boy named Roy moved in next door.
>
> He had few friends. Troy let him use his drum. The boy shouted with joy.
> *Example:* **toy, Troy, tom-tom, boy, joy.**

253. Verbs or action words may be taught by using picture clues. A picture showing some act being performed is accompanied by three words, only one describing the action in the picture. The child matches the word with the picture by drawing a circle around the correct response. Pictures may illustrate actions such as **hop, swim** or **ride.**

254. As an introduction to crossword puzzles, the following exercise may be used. The child is given a definition of a word. Alongside it, the beginning letter is supplied and the correct number of spaces for the remaining letters. He completes the correct word.

Example:

1. in the middle of the day | n | o | o | n |

(noon)

255. Give students several sentences using the same word but in different meanings. The definitions for the word may be numbered under the sentences, and the student answers by filling in each blank with the proper number.

Example:

Mary liked to **draw** pictures. ___

Father went to the bank to **draw** out some money. ___

The bridge could not open because the **draw** was stuck. ___

1. The movable part of a drawbridge.
2. The act, process or result of drawing.
3. To take (money) from a place of deposit.

256. Stories may be duplicated about the cowboy's life in the Old West, space travel or other unit material for review. Terms related to the subject are omitted, and the students read the story and fill in the blanks with the correct terms. This may be done as a game with a small group, or the stories may be put on acetate sheets and used over and over again. Part of a story may run like this:

In the Old West cowboys lived on the (**range, prairie**). To be sure each rancher knew his own cattle, he burned his (**brand**) on each cow. This was done during the spring of the year at (**roundup**) time. Newborn calves would be (**lassoed**) and (**branded**) with a hot iron.

VARIATION: Every fifth word in any story can be covered.

257. Have students select five words from the glossary of a book used by the class. They write five sentences, omitting the chosen word in each one. They read the sentences to the group. The other students try to guess the missing words from the context and from previous reading in the book.

258. Display some pictures of food. Place flash cards with the name of each food in an envelope. On the outside of the envelope, print sentences concerning the pictures. Have students take the words out of the envelope and use them to fill in the sentences.

1. See the juicy _____.
2. The _____ is hot.
3. There are four _____.

259. Sentences and words from the textbook are used to strengthen meaning from the context. These may be done on charts or board, or they may be duplicated.

Example: Read the following sentence and answer the questions given below:

1. The boy walked briskly down the winding path.
   Which word tells you how the boy walked?
   Which word tells you the path was not straight?

260. The child must be trained to use context to unlock a new word, rather than guessing. For practice in this area, several sentences may be written, leaving out an important word in each one. The new words should be read in context for checking purposes.

For example:

(The new words: **punctuate, infirmity**)

1. Be sure to _____ the sentence by putting in the commas and period.
2. Mr. Jones's _____ was caused by his recent sickness.

261. Practice in context reading should include multiple-choice sentences that include initial and medial letter differences. This will help children focus their attention on the total word.

For example:

The lady wears a (hut, hat, let) to church.

Sentence Structure—*Word Position, Figures of Speech, Words Used as Noun, Verb (Word Functions)*

262. The teacher prepares cards, each bearing one word of a sentence. Each child is given a card, and they are placed in line so the sentence may be read correctly. One child is asked to sit down, and the sentence is reread without the omitted word. This helps children discover the importance of a word to the structure of the sentence. The missing word may even change the meaning of a sentence.

This technique may be used to construct sentences. The cards are given out, and the child who has the first word comes to the front. The child who thinks he has the second word joins him, and they continue until the sentence is correctly constructed.

263. Write several words on the board which you will omit when reading a story to the class. As you read the story, pause where a word has been omitted. Members of the group take turns telling which word on the board should go in the blank space.

264. After the group has read a story silently, direct their attention to sentences which contain pronouns. Students name each pronoun and tell the person, place or thing to which it refers.

265. Write sentences on the board in which the words have been arranged in mixed order. Have the students read each sentence, and underline the word which would come first when the sentence is in its proper order. Be sure your sentences are pertinent to the children's interests and, if possible, use their names in the sentences.

Examples:

    1. went <u>Sue</u> the zoo Mother and to.

    2. outside to went <u>Bill</u> play.

    3. is name your <u>What</u>?

266. Give children sentences containing words in jumbled order. Have the children rewrite the sentences correctly and state whether each one is true or false.

For example:

    1. Grow maple orange trees on.

The child's response should be:

    1. Oranges grow on maple trees. *False.*

267. List eight or ten action words on the board or in a pocket chart. A child is picked to come to the front of the room and act out one of the action words. By observing the action, children in the group take turns trying to determine the word being used.

268. Several sentences, each containing an omitted word, are mounted on a flannel board. An envelope containing plural and singular forms of nouns, adverbs, adjectives, various ending forms and tenses is provided. The child selects an appropriate word form to complete the sentence and places his response on the flannel board.

269. Phrases or idiomatic expressions taken from the text may be written on the overhead projector or duplicated. The students give the meanings either orally or written.

Examples:

He was "cross as a bear" means ⎯⎯⎯⎯⎯⎯⎯⎯⎯⎯.
"Happy as a lark" means ⎯⎯⎯⎯⎯⎯⎯⎯⎯.

270. Write some sentences or a short story on the board. Students read them and find the most important word in each sentence. Underline this topic word. Then, erase everything but the topic words. Selecting one of the words, have the student verbally reconstruct the sentence from which it came.

271. Divide the board into sections. In each section, draw a picture illustrating a prepositional phrase. Also, print a question in each section concerning the picture. Discuss the picture. A student answers the ques-

tion using a complete sentence. Either the teacher or student may write his response in the corresponding square.

272. Advertisements use figures of speech effectively to sell their products. Collect old magazines and newspapers for use in the classroom. Groups may be appointed to look for metaphors, similes or personifications within ads. These may be mounted on charts to display the various ways figures of speech can be applied effectively.

Chapter Five

LANGUAGE DEVELOPMENT
AND VOCABULARY

I. ORAL COMMUNICATION

Rationale

In ever-increasing numbers, reading specialists are recognizing the relevance of the development of the child's language skills for reading success. Classroom teachers are realizing that learning to read is more than simply saying the words of the reader. Children cannot really learn to read, in the sense that reading is thinking with words, unless their own language skills are well developed—in other words, unless they can first use words in meaningful ways. Reading progress is limited when children use baby talk, or substitute one sound for another. It is almost impossible when they cannot mentally frame sentences to express what they wish to say, or these ideas are offered in fragments or rudimentary strings of words. Reading continues to be memorized word-naming, if the structure of the printed sentences or the ideas they offer are more advanced than the child's own language or his idea background.

The reading program must supply the experiences, or the *ideas*, which may be translated into words—the medium of the reading act. Printed words are only symbols for ideas and concepts which, in turn, are familiar or not according to the experiences of the reader. Reading words is not an end in itself but the amalgamation of the reader's thinking or language ability and first-hand experiences with the concepts offered by the author.

BEHAVIORAL OUTCOMES

The child will learn to:

> speak largely in complete thoughts or sentences
>
> be familiar with various patterns of sentences in speech, in printed matter and auditorily
>
> vary his inflection or intonation within a sentence in keeping with the purpose of the sentence
>
> develop a growing stock of ideas (words) based upon first-hand experiences
>
> recognize relationships among the ideas expressed by words
>
> understand the dialectal speech of his teacher and peers
>
> grow in ability to express his own ideas in various ways in an effort to communicate

Communication—Group Activities, Individual Activities

273. *Hint:* Read selections related to the content of the current unit or story in parallel readers of the same series, other basal readers, trade books or literary readers correlated with the basal reader.

274. Children are encouraged to bring collections, toys or personal possessions to class for sharing. The teacher allows the child time to share his experience or object and tell all he can about it. This strengthens oral communication and helps the child feel an important part of his classroom environment. Sharing with a large group is effective for a short period of time, and general evaluation follows.

275. Two classes can work up an exchange program. Each week, one student prepares a story to read to another class and someone from that class prepares to read one to your class. This provides children an opportunity to read orally before a group of strangers. Each child is given an opportunity to participate.

276. One section of the board is set aside for sharing classroom news. Children who have something to share may write it on paper, discuss needed corrections with the teacher, then write the news on the board. At the end of the day the news is read aloud. As a penmanship lesson the news is written and a paper selected to go in a binder labeled "Class News." A booklet may be kept for the entire year to relate important class news. The class may wish to make a news board to be situated outside their room. They may post their room news, school news, community information or important events from the newspapers (moon launch, opening of shopping center) for all to enjoy.

Interpretation

277. List sentences on the board which require a variety of expressions. Select a child to read a sentence to himself. Encourage him to determine if the sentence is exciting, sad or a question. After he has analyzed it, he reads it, using his voice to show the feeling expressed in the sentence.

Examples:

1. "What is your favorite story?"
2. "This is my wagon."
3. "David! Come here right now!"
4. "I don't feel like playing."

278. There are many sources of stories and poems which are adaptable to choral reading. Make use of these sources and techniques to develop skills in interpretation, fluency and inflection (besides, it's fun!).

Fluency, Inflection

279. Choosing a simple exclamation such as "oh," students respond with the inflection needed to react to the following statements:

1. Someone stepped on your toe.
2. You see just what you wanted under the Christmas tree.
3. You just heard some surprising news.

4. There will be no school tomorrow.
5. We will have school this Saturday.

280. In reading a sentence, we break it into parts or phrases.

For example:

Joe went into the house to find Mother.

Joe went   into the house   to find Mother.

Make a set of flash cards, each showing a group of words naturally phrased together when read aloud.

For example:

1. in the tree
2. down the road
3. saw them coming
4. up the stairs

Practice saying words in phrases will help children read more smoothly and quickly. Hold each card up, one at a time. Allow about three seconds, then put the card down and call on someone to tell what the card said. Tell the students to watch carefully, for they will have to make their eyes read quickly.

281. Read a sentence, emphasizing a different word each time. Students interpret the change of emphasis as each word is stressed.

FOLLOW-UP: students compose sentences and read them aloud to the small group, using these patterns of emphasis.

Example: This is my lunch. What are you doing here?

II. BUILDING SIGHT AND MEANING VOCABULARY

Rationale

It is not a new concept that word recognition is the fundamental basis of all reading development. But, by some, this recognition has been interpreted to mean word-naming or word-calling, thus losing sight of the fact that words are simply ideas, or ways of expressing ideas. Words may be the bricks in the building of reading, but word meanings and relationships are the mortar that holds the bricks together. The learner must realize that words do not have a single meaning or a single function in a sentence. Even apparently simple words are not learned by sheer repetition, particularly in drills in isolation or lists, for often even these simple words have multiple meanings and usage. Nor are words learned solely through reading experience, for their understanding depends upon auditory, vocal and writing experiences. Words are really a group of ideas associated with a central thought, and their true understanding demands practice in learning relationships among and between ideas (words).

BEHAVIORAL OUTCOMES

The child will learn:

to categorize and classify words according to their meanings

to distinguish the relationships among homonyms, synonyms and antonyms

to deal with the multiple meanings and usage of words

to broaden and deepen his word associations by using qualifying and descriptive words

Categorizing and Classifying Words

282. The children draw or cut pictures of pets, food or other objects from magazines. A series of charts is made, each one bearing a different heading, such as "Things We Eat," or "Animals We Like." The children sort and classify the pictures, matching them with the appropriate charts. Instead of making large charts, each child may make an individual dictionary of classified objects.

283. Make a hen and eggs from construction or colored poster paper. You can put words or pictures on the eggs that have to do with things found on a farm. Some of the eggs should show things which do *not* belong on a farm. The child classifies words pertaining to a farm by slipping the proper eggs behind the hen.

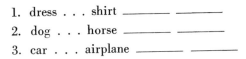

284. The following exercise is written on the board or on a chart. The students look at the first two words in each line, then list two additional words which belong to the same category. They may use the dictionary or word list in the back of their readers for help.

      1. dress . . . shirt _____ _____
      2. dog . . . horse _____ _____
      3. car . . . airplane _____ _____

285. At the top of a sheet of oaktag, print the names or pictures of several kinds of stores (toy store, shoe store, clothing store). Under the name of each store, make a list of some items you could buy there. Cut the lists apart and put them in different envelopes. The children try to match the articles with the correct store headings. If desired, the stores and lists could be made from felt or backed with flannel to use on the flannel board.

286. To review vocabulary and idea classification, the following exercise may be written on large sheets of newsprint. The child reads the question and illustrates possible answers.

      What's the answer?
      1. What is fun to ride in?
      2. What is good to eat?

287. Alphabetizing may be used for many things, including foods. Each player gives the name of a food beginning with a new letter of the alphabet. He names a food starting with **A,** such as apples; the next person, **B,** and so on. Help may be given for letters such as **Q, U, X** or **Z.** Quail, quaker oats, upside-down cake or zucchini may be used.

288. The child is given a list of words and follows two sets of directions.
   Example: Draw a ring around the things you wear. Put two lines under the things you do.

coat	shirt	dress
walk	play	shoes
swim	run	hat

289. Sheets of paper are labeled by classification headings. Each child maintains his own folder of topics to add to as new words are met in his independent reading. Headings would vary with pupils' work levels.

Examples:

Color words	Words that describe something
Shape words	Words for how people feel

Family words	Words for how people look
Ways people can move	Words for kinds of talk
Doing words	Homes for people
Size words	Substitutes for people's names (pronouns)

These vocabulary sheets are very helpful during creative writing, to aid in spelling as well as to increase descriptive writing.

290. New words from children's experience stories or any reading material are written on small cards, approximately 1x2 inches. The pupil files these in a small box alphabetically. Many activities can be developed using the boxes of words.

Example: During activity period, a group of students place their **A** through **D** words on their desk, word side up. When the leader asks for a category of words, the students hold up their words which apply, reading them aloud when called on. This activity brings about much involvement and helps students to react quickly. Categories from Activity No. 289 can be used, plus many from other areas of the curriculum; i.e., number words, weather words, animals or transportation.

291. List several directions on the board for children to read, write and follow. List the directions, and under each give several choices. Children circle their responses according to the instructions.

Examples:

1. Find two ways of travel.
    plane   can   car   flower
2. Find two flowers.
    road   daisy   violet   pen

292. This game encourages the children to classify household items. The teacher prepares word cards using the names of items that can be found in a house. She distributes these cards, then asks for items found in a certain room or place. The children then put the items called for in the van. The van may be a toy truck or any suitable container.

293. Make two columns of proper and common nouns. Have students indicate whether each noun is a person, place or thing.

Examples:

1. Sally—person
2. cap—thing
3. Jacksonville—place
4. brother—person
5. umbrella—thing
6. Florida—place
7. nickel—thing
8. John—person

This could be made more difficult by having students indicate why, what and where.

Examples:

1. in the house—where
2. he was afraid—why
3. on the tree—where
4. in the yard—where
5. it was raining—why
6. the bell—what
7. by the gate—where
8. the dog—what

294. Give each child a duplicated sheet containing ten rows of words, four words in each row. Each row of words should contain the names of such categories as colors, items of furniture, animals or flowers. The teacher should give directions slowly, but only once. She will give progressively more involved directions for succeeding rows. To begin, she will say, "Circle the name of an item of furniture" in row one. Then, in row two, "Draw a line under the name of a color and mark an **X** through the name of an animal."

1. purple; table, sheep, daisy
2. green, chair, horse, lily
3. blue, bed, lion, tulip

295. Formulate a list of words that can be classified into different groups. Classification headings are given, and the children try to arrange the words into the proper groupings.

Example:

wagon	FRUIT	PETS	TOYS
peach	peach	dog	wagon
train	grape	cat	train
grape			
dog			
cat			

296. Children make individual notebooks for words concerning subjects that interest them. They may categorize them under headings such as:

Space words: capsule, orbit, experiments

Funny words: joke, humorous, comical

Action words: skip, gallop, ran

Neighborhood words: streets, buildings, upkeep, private property

297. Give each child a duplicated copy of words pertaining to a particular classification, whose spellings have been scrambled. Allow a limited time for students to unscramble the words and write their correct spellings on another sheet of paper. The winner is the one with the most unscrambled words rewritten correctly. For poor spellers, a word list might be supplied.

Example:

TYPES OF SHELTER

1. Eskimo home (ilogo)   igloo
2. Indian home (ntte)   tent
3. Early man's home (vcea)   cave
4. City dweller's home (tnemaptar)   apartment
5. Traveler's home (letho)   hotel

298. The teacher lists several vocabulary words on the board. Some of the words are appropriate to a particular type of story. The children are asked to indicate the words that could be used for that type of story.

For example:

HALLOWE'EN

ghost	bats	rope	cows
cowboy	river	airplane	broom
city	jack-o'-lanterns	horse	bullet

They may be asked to select the words appropriate for use in a Hallowe'en story.

299. Divide the class into two teams, each player having a pencil, paper and a dictionary. The players divide their papers into three columns, as shown below, and label the columns "Food," "Clothing," "Shelter."

The teacher then writes on the chalkboard a list of unfamiliar words that can be definitely categorized, such as **asparagus, cathedral, surplice, succotash, sari, gazebo.**

Students are to use their dictionaries to determine the correct column in which to write each word. A point is scored for each word correctly placed; the team with the most points wins the game.

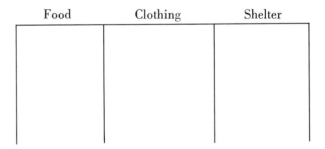

Food	Clothing	Shelter

300. Write on the chalkboard the words **mouth, eyes** and **feet,** as labels for three columns. On the side of the board, write a list of words, such as **lope, warble, sashay, peruse, vocalize, scrutinize** and **harangue.** Ask students, for example, whether one lopes with his mouth, eyes or feet. Then, have children locate each word in the dictionary, reading all the definitions given, to determine in which category the word belongs.

301. Choose topics such as wood, glass, plastic or metal. Go around the room, giving each child a turn to name an object made from the material chosen. He may not duplicate something already given. If he is unable to think of a new word, he is "out."

302. A scrambled bulletin board is an excellent way to introduce new vocabulary words to be used in a unit. This may be used with science, social studies units or language arts areas such as syllables, compound words, rhyming words, antonyms, homonyms, synonyms, prefixes or suffixes. The words "Scrambled Board" are written diagonally across the board. The words being used are divided into two sections. Below the board, display items that will be used in the unit of study. If it is being used as a language board, pictures or charts with related words may accompany the display. An example of a science board is as follows:

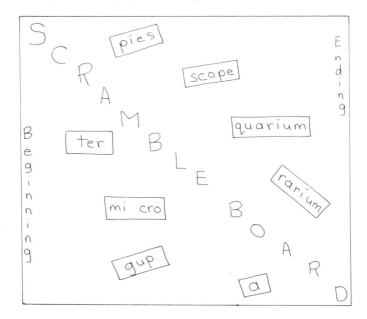

Words used	*Items to accompany board*	
aquarium	aquarium	gravel
microscope	pond water	microscope
terrarium	net	plants
guppies	fish	
	guppies	

303. Change only one letter in each word to make words related to water. Letters may also change position.

sew	(wet, sea)	fond	creel
halls		gull	tool
lane		fill	wall
muddle		ray	streak

Homonyms, Synonyms, Antonyms

304. The child is given two lists of words written in parallel columns. He indicates **s** between the two words if the meanings are similar, and **d** if they are different.

For example:

front	(d)	out
large	(s)	enormous
day	(d)	night
beside	(s)	near

305. Give each student a duplicated copy of such words as the following, which have homonyms. Have the class give another spelling and definition for each word.

1. fare	6. maid
2. sight	7. night
3. plane	8. piece
4. rein	9. write
5. cent	10. led

306. Definitions are given that call for double homonym answers. Students read the definitions and try to figure out the homonym pairs needed to complete the answers.

1. oh	owe—Response to the bill collector.
2. male	mail—Man who delivers letters.
3. pain	pane—Cracked window.
4. see	sea—Look at ocean.
5. roam	Rome—To wander about a city in Italy.

307. Several words may be listed or duplicated, and the students asked to list synonyms, antonyms or both for each given word.

Examples:

List three synonyms for each of these words:

1. pleasant   _____   _____   _____
2. brutal   _____   _____   _____

List three antonyms for each of these words:

1. happy   _____   _____   _____
2. simple   _____   _____   _____

List an antonym and a synonym for each of these words:

	antonym	*synonym*
1. wet	_____	_____
2. tall	_____	_____

308. Give every child a dictionary. Then, give challenges, such as:

"How many synonyms for **fast** can you find?" "How many for **run**?" "How many for **talk**?"

What is the preferred pronunciation of **envelope?**

How many meanings for the word **joint** can you find?

309. The child is given a paragraph containing many overused words. Substitute words are listed. The child is asked to replace the overworked words with ones from the substitute list, by listing them below the original words. More able students will not need a list.

Example:

Tom *walked* through the woods. He saw a squirrel *hurrying* up a tree.

strolled   scampering

sauntered   scurrying

310. Several words are listed and numbered. The opposites of each are written in a column beside the given words but in mixed order. Parentheses are placed in front of the opposites, allowing space to indicate the numbers of the antonyms. Use some words that don't match.

Examples:

1. beautiful	( )	cold
2. morning	(1)	ugly
3. hot	( )	close
4. near	( )	evening

11. List some words in a column. To the right of each word, give three ldditional words, one of which is the opposite in meaning of the first ord. The child is to circle the antonym in each row.

mean	kind	cruel	near
hungry	famished	saturated	salivate

12. List some words on the board. Students give an antonym for each. This may be done orally or as a written exercise.

Examples:

sweet	last
play	late
new	difficult
short	large

13. Homonyms and word pairs that are often confused may be pre- nted together. The students are to look up the meanings and use the ords in sentences. Some of the pairs could be: **chews, choose; rough, threw; flower, flour; rein, rain.** This activity may be ied orally or written.

14. Homonym Contest. Teams of two students find as many pairs of monyms as they can from many sources. Each valid pair counts one)int. Deduct five points for invalid pairs. For the ground rules, a valid ir would be words that are *pronounced* alike but *spelled* differently, ith different *meanings*. Identical phonetic respellings in the dictionary)uld determine like pronunciations. A full week should be given for search. A committee would screen the papers to determine the winning am.

Multiple Meanings of Words and Usage

315. The children are arranged in a circle, leaving sufficient space around the outside for an outer circle. Each child in the group is asked a question by the teacher or a leader. If he fails to respond correctly, he leaves the inner circle and moves to the outside circle. The child who remains to the end without missing is the winner. The winner then calls on each person in the outer circle (the losers) and asks them questions previously missed.

For example:

What is a baby cat called?   (kitten)

What is another word for **pal**?   (friend)

What kind of glass makes objects look larger?   (magnifying glass)

316. Give each student a duplicated crossword puzzle sheet. When puzzles are first introduced, use puzzles with answers written across only. Later, the traditional crossword puzzle with answers written both across and down may be employed.

An example of a simple puzzle:

1. It says, "mew, mew."
2. To see.
3. The opposite of "sad."
4. The first school day of the week.
5. A boy is "he," the girl is ___.
6. A place where many animals live.
7. This animal has a trunk.

317. Students can come up with original ideas for describing intangible terms. Use this activity as a creative writing lesson. Be sure all the students understand what kinds of noun forms qualify as intangibles. Have them see how many original ideas they can think of. Crayon illustrations may also be made, for further enrichment. Nouns such as the following may be used:

Happiness is _____

Love is _____

Misery is _____

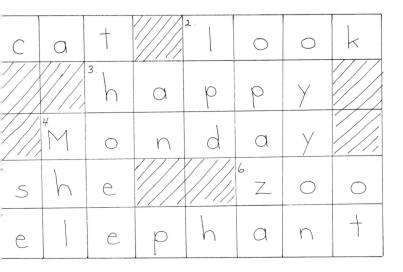

18. Divide the class into two teams and provide a red tag for one _am, a blue tag for the other. Use a playing board similar to a baseball _amond. The game begins with both tags on home plate. The teacher _ts as pitcher, giving each player a word which he must pronounce _d use in a sentence concerning baseball. If the player uses his word _rrectly, his team's tag is moved from home to first base. If the next _ayer fails, he is "out" and the first tag remains at its present base. _fter three "outs," the other team comes to bat. Teams take turns pro-_ouncing and using a word in a sentence. One run is scored each time _e team tag rounds the bases and returns to home plate.

19. Divide the board or paper into four columns. Label each column _ follows:

Root Word   Present—Now   Past—Yesterday   Future—Tomorrow

_ the first column, list root words which are conjugated by adding _dings or helping words to show changes in tense. Have pupils add _eeded endings or helping words to the base words to show things that _appen now, things that happened yesterday or things that may happen _morrow.

Example:

Root Word	*Present*	*Past*	*Future*
1. work	he is working	he worked	he will work

320. Make small flashcards, 2x3 inches. On each, write a vocabulary word being used in reading, science or social studies. Make a corresponding number of cards, 2x6 inches; on each, write a definition for one of the vocabulary words. Have students place the cards on their desks and match each word with its definition. If desired, the words may be written in one color and the definitions in another. A checksheet may be made, or the correct words may be printed on the back of the definition cards for self-correction.

scale	guide to interpret map information, scale, symbols
cardinal point	representative figures standing for objects shown on a map
symbols	one of the four principal compass points: north, south, east, west
key	a divided line on a map indicating the length used to represent a larger unit of measure

321. Fun with Homographs. Start the group with a few words which have multiple meanings and origins, but which are pronounced and spelled alike. Discuss the many meanings orally. Then, the children must search throughout the week for additional concepts and patterns of use. At the end of the week, students may bring in their lists for further discussion.

Examples:

> **run** (speed, stockings, kennel, river, nose, election)
> **fair** (complexion, just, display)
> **fast** (speed, not eat, secure)
> **bar** (guard against, saloon, solid material)

322. The teacher and pupils may make a chart together of words which may disappear from our language some day. These should be discussed, and reasons given for their diminishing usage.

Examples:

sneakers	bloomers	leggings
slip-ons	mules	shay

323. Use word squares that read the same vertically and horizontally to develop word meaning. Enclose the puzzle in an acetate folder. Give clues for numbered squares, the same way as in regular crossword puzzles. Students should make up their own acrostic puzzles.

Across and Down:

1. A mass of flames
2. To smooth out
3. Synonym for street
4. Opposite of "begins"

324. Direct students' attention to words of similar visual detail: **accept, except; went, want; from, form; prescribe, subscribe.** Ask students to list other groups of words which at a glance appear alike but have different spellings and definitions.

FOLLOW-UP: Give each child a duplicated copy of sentences such as these, and have him cross out the incorrect word and write in the proper one:

The whether map predicted a storm.

My mother prescribes to several magazines.

She excepted the invitation to my party.

325. Give each student a duplicated copy of puzzles in which only the first letter of a word and the correct number of spaces for the other letters are given.

Direct the class to fill in the correct words.

Examples:

1. a day set aside to celebrate an event. h_____ (holiday)
2. free, unoccupied time for rest or recreation. l_____ (leisure)
3. gaiety, gladness or great amusement. m_____ (mirth)
4. to obtain by paying a price. p_____ (purchase)

326. Add one letter to the first letter to make a two-letter word; then, add two letters, and so on.

i__	opposite of out (in)	a__	short for advertisement (ad)
__i__	opposite of stand (sit)	__a__	unhappy (sad)
__i__	half of a pair (twin)		
__i__	a pleasant grin (smile)		

327. To check the frequent usage of basic sight words such as **it, this, that, is, was, I, the** and **you,** have students analyze original essays or stories. By counting these words as they appear, a tally may be kept to determine the frequency of word usage. The count may be kept as a weekly tally for the class or a small group. A chart may also be used to record the data. This type of activity can also serve as an introduction to percentages and averages in graphs.

Word Frequency

name	*it*	*this*	*that*	*is*	*the*
Susan	7	8	5	11	10
Bill	8	4	3	7	6
Ted	3	6	2	6	12
Debbie	9	5	9	6	9
	—	—	—	—	—
	27	23	19	30	37
Averages:	6.75	5.75	4.75	7.5	8.75

328. The children read an assigned story, then list words that express time, place and cause. These words should be listed under their correct columns. This may be done as a small group activity; allow time for discussion and evaluation.

329. Provide each child with a ditto of blank squares similar to the example shown below. Instruct students to "climb the steps" by filling in each step, working from the bottom up, with the answer suggested by the corresponding clue. As each child finishes, he may check his answers with the master copy. Different categories may be used, depending on the subjects currently being studied; *for example:* inventions, states or bodies of water.

1. Its flag is the Union Jack.
2. The country bordering the U.S. on the north.
3. An Asian country once a British possession.
4. An island country ruled by a dictator.
5. The abbreviation for United States of America.

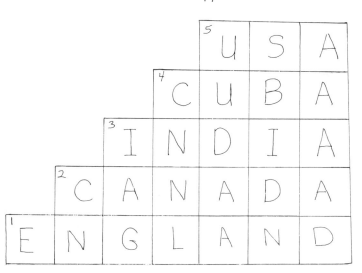

Master Copy

330. Children are encouraged to analyze new words they do not know for pronunciation and meaning. Often this can be very misleading. For example, the word **jailbird** might refer to a bird in prison. List several words the meanings of which may be misinterpreted if analyzed part by part. Logical but incorrect meanings may be listed in a second column. Have students match the words with the definitions and describe the logic behind each meaning. Students add new words as they are able.

lettuce	asking permission to do something
groovy	deep ridges
carpetbagger	one who wraps carpets

331. Direct students to choose a noun and write it vertically on their papers, one letter beneath the other. Then, have them make adjectives that will describe the noun, using each of the letters in the noun.

Example:

H . . . hairy
O . . . ornery
R . . . reliable
S . . . silky
E . . . energetic

332. Give each student a duplicated copy of fifteen words and ten sentences in which words have been omitted. Have the students choose the correct word to complete each sentence. There will be five words left over.

plague	circumference	consequence
typhoon	precaution	biology
serene	astronomy	tropical
talons	grotesque	tycoon
illustrations	industrious	duplicate

1. The eagle sank his _____ into the wildcat.
2. The distance around a circle is called its _____.
3. _____ is the study of the heavenly bodies.
4. _____ is the study of animal life.
5. A _____ is a violent storm.
6. The _____ for the book were done by a noted artist.
7. The Hunchback of Notre Dame was a _____ figure.

8. Muddy roads are a _____ of heavy rains.
9. An _____ student usually makes good grades.
10. Bananas and coconuts grow most abundantly in _____ climates.

Qualifying or Descriptive Words

333. Action and descriptive words are introduced with primary children. Sentences are written on the board, omitting the action or descriptive words. The class discusses all the ways a person may do something or how he may look. Several possible action words may be listed as they are discussed. The same thing may be done with descriptive words. The children then write the sentences and select an appropriate word to complete each one. They may illustrate the sentences to show how picture words affect them.

Example:

The horse _____ down the lane.

334. Write on chalkboard or transparency, in sequence, such phrases as **the house, the white house, the large white house, the large white house with green shutters.** Encourage students to describe how the addition of each descriptive phrase alters the image of the first phrase.

FOLLOW-UP: As an individual activity, give each student a duplicated copy of such undefined phrases as **a boat, the horse, a table** and **the zoo,** and have him expand each phrase by adding as many descriptive phrases as possible.

335. Students may illustrate something smooth, something soft, something rough or something pretty.

336. To identify and describe sounds, have students close their eyes while one student performs an action that entails a definite sound, such as sharpening a pencil or knocking on a door. After the sound has been identified, ask the class to suggest words that most accurately describe the sound.

FOLLOW-UP: Select a story with vivid auditory images. Divide the class into groups, and instruct each group to tell the story using only sound effects to relate the action.

337. Pictures or objects may be used to convey meanings of descriptive words such as **shiny, dull, thick** and **thin,** or abstract words such as **off** or **on.** The teacher holds up an object and asks the children to give words that describe it, such as **round** or **heavy.** With abstract words, a picture showing leaves on the ground and others on the tree may be used to elicit the words **blew off.** Further questioning will strengthen the concept of "off" and "on."

Another way to elicit descriptive words is by having an "Apple Party." Each child brings a small apple to school. Observe the apple and list as many words as possible to describe its appearance **(red, shiny, slick)**; then, eat the apple and add additional words to your vocabulary list **(delicious, sweet, juicy).** The class may then write stories telling about their "Apple Party" and have many descriptive words available for use. The stories may be attractively displayed on red construction paper with apple cutouts.

338. Bring an imaginary box, full of presents, into the room. Each child reaches into the "box," picks a present, unwraps it and begins describing it to the group. The other children try to guess the imaginary object from the description given.

339. Action words are listed on the board. Sentences are given, and the children complete each by using the action verb denoting the appropriate motion for that sentence.

limped	raced
skipped	walked
hopped	staggered

In an effort to win, the boy _____ down the field.

His paw hurt, the dog _____ to his master.

340. After discussing the importance of descriptive and action words in evoking definite sensory images, choose such words from a story the class has just read; for example: **boiling, stormy, winding, hissing.** List them on the chalkboard, and have students explain what image each of the words brings to mind.

Encourage children to find other such words in their books and to describe the images each word calls to mind.

341. After using various playground equipment, ask students to list action words that tell about the experiences they had. They may come up with words such as **slide fast, throw quickly** or **swing high.**

342. Analyze commercials and advertisements to see why they are appealing. Discuss color, arrangement and descriptive writing to find what gets their attention. Point up interesting word usage, vivid language or imagery. Have students write word pictures and phrases to describe a favorite product.

343. The children are given a copy of an adventure story which has been previously read. They underline any phrases, words or events which create excitement or make word pictures. A completed paragraph may look like this:

> The cowboy sat <u>astride his horse</u>, his lasso <u>entangled</u> in the horns of the <u>angry</u> bull. Suddenly the <u>bull twisted in rage</u>. The horse <u>reared</u> to tighten the rope. With a final <u>jerk</u> of the rope, the bull was <u>thrown off his feet</u> and the cowboy quickly <u>bound</u> his hooves.

344. Divide the class into two teams. Pronounce slowly, and only once, three such descriptive words as **enormous, winding, shadowy.** Then, direct a player to give three sentences, using one of the words in each sentence.

Teams alternate making sentences; the team with the most points is the winner.

Chapter Six

LOCATION SKILLS

Rationale

Although it is often lost sight of in the reading program, our greatest goal is to produce independent readers—individuals who can use reading for their own life purposes. Independence in reading demands skill in using books and other resource materials. Among the most frequently used resources are the dictionary and the library, and development of skill in their use is an essential part of the reading program.

Many pupils never learn to use the dictionary for any other value than the meaning of a difficult word. They fail to attend to the information given regarding pronunciation, derivation or usage. Because of the lack of these associations, they often fail to retain the meanings of the words and the dictionary becomes simply a momentary aid. Many of the library skills that must be learned are quite mechanical, and their practice is often divorced from actual library use. For these reasons, many pupils never realize the values of a library, and seldom use it in after-school life.

We have tried to recognize some of these instructional deficiencies in outlining activities in these areas. But the task of making these learnings vital and functional depends upon the manner and setting in which they occur. Whenever possible, these activities should include actual use of the dictionary or the library.

BEHAVIORAL OUTCOMES

The child will learn to:

> use the alphabetic arrangement of the dictionary
>
> use the guide words of the dictionary
>
> interpret the pronunciation key
>
> derive meanings suited to a context for difficult words
>
> understand usage terms and abbreviations
>
> utilize aids in a book, such as the index and the table of contents
>
> employ the card catalog in finding books
>
> become familiar with the resources of a library

I. DICTIONARY SKILLS

Alphabetic Sequence and Approximate Place of Letter in Alphabet (e.g., Middle or Last Quarter)

345. Flannel letters may be used for practice in alphabetizing. Capital and lowercase letters may be made from flannel or cardboard. If cardboard is used, each letter should be backed with soft cloth or sandpaper so the letters will stick to the flannelboard. This is a meaningful independent activity.

346. A large clock face is made from cardboard. Attach a movable hand and number the clock face from one to twelve. On the board or a card, list twelve different alphabet series. Each child spins the hand of the clock to see on which number it will land. He reads the corresponding series of alphabet letters in their correct order.

Example of alphabet series:

1. b, d, c	4. m, l, n
2. t, s, r	5. r, q, p
3. y, z, x	6. g, e, f

347. A hose box is turned into a practice game for learning alphabetical order. Mark off twenty-six equal squares into the bottom and top of the box and cut out the same number of squares, slightly smaller, from stiff paper. Print a different letter on each square. Capitals may be on one side, and lowercase letters on the other. Children arrange the letters in proper sequence in the box. A duplicate board may be made in the lid of the box and used as a checking key.

348. The alphabet is printed in proper sequence on a large piece of cardboard. The board is cut into pieces to make a puzzle. The children put the puzzle together. If desired, the puzzle may be made from masonite, cutting the pieces with a jigsaw. The letters could be painted on or formed with heavy tape.

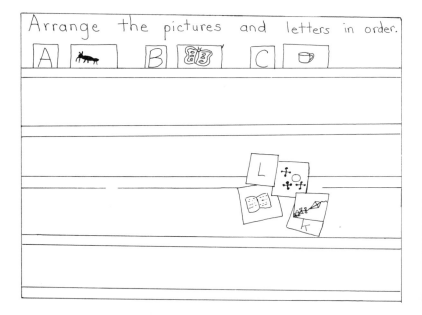

349. On the board, specify categories such as **countries, foods** and **animals.** Students copy the headings and list items under each one, beginning with as many different letters as they can. Words should be written in alphabetic sequence.

    Example:

        Countries

        Austria

        Belgium

        Cuba

350. To aid a child in using a dictionary or index effectively, drill in alphabetizing is helpful. Such questions can be used as, "What letter comes before **s, f**?" or, "What letter comes after **u, i**?" The child may also be asked to arrange a series of letters or names in alphabetical order.

For example: **t, s, l, o, p** should be rewritten **l, o, p, s, t.**

351. Promote vocabulary development by challenging students to organize words according to alphabetical order. Using reading vocabulary, have students find words in the story that begin with each letter of the alphabet, locate descriptive words beginning with each letter of the alphabet or find words to introduce or conclude conversation that begin with each letter of the alphabet. Alphabet booklets may be made, using words from unit studies such as:

Famous people in history	Fiction characters
Space	Animals

Since children should be given time to write at the chalkboard, the lists may be written rather than made into book form. After the answers have been given, the child may share the learning experience with a small group. Students may also practice writing words, sentences, stories or letters on the board.

352. The first child in the group says a word, and the next person must give a word beginning with the second letter of the preceding word. Each correct word earns a small colored square of paper. The child having the most color tabs at the end wins the game.

Examples: cab, antelope, number, useful, sister.

353. Each letter of the alphabet is printed on three cards, giving a total of seventy-eight cards. All cards should be the same size (about 3x4). Each of four players is dealt six cards, and the remaining cards are placed facedown on the table. Each child takes his turn drawing a card and playing. The object is to form a four-card run in sequence (such as **b-c-d-e**). He may play the cards down in front of him and draw from the pile until he draws a card he cannot play. A child may also build a letter sequence by adding to a set already played. The child playing the most cards at the end of the game wins.

354. List words on the board taken from the dictionary. Have students locate each word and write the word that precedes or follows the given word.

355. Secret messages are an effective and pleasant means of practicing alphabet sequence.

On the chalkboard, write a message in secret code. Use simple codes, such as the next letter in the alphabet in place of the desired letter, or the number of the letter as it appears in the alphabet. The students decipher the code, then follow the directions of the message.

Example:

s b j t f   z p v s   i b o e   "Raise Your Hand"

18 1 9 19 5   25 15 21 18   8 1 14 4

356. A small group may practice using the dictionary by having a word drill. Choose various types of information to be found. The leader calls for a word or specific information to be found. The first one to locate the answer gets a point.

1. locate a word
2. find the definition
3. give the preferred pronunciation
4. give the diacritical markings

Alphabetizing by First Letter, First Two or Three

357. The names of the boys and girls in the class may be used as an exercise in alphabetical order. List several names on the board. Have students rearrange the names in alphabetical order according to the first name.

Jane Cunningham	Rex Johns	Tommy Douglas
Barbara Jenkins	Ann Jackson	Mike Cox

358. The teacher may print a capital letter on the board and ask each child whose last name begins with that letter to write his name on the board. For example, the letter **C** may be given and all children whose last names begin with **C** go to the board and write their name. A discussion should follow to determine which name should be first and the appropriate order for each one. This method may also be used in corollating famous literature or social studies names.

359. Write a list of words on the board for the children to arrange in alphabetical order. The words may be taken from objects in the room, from a page in the reader or from the child's personal chart vocabulary.

360. A room telephone directory may be compiled by a small group or the entire class. Be sure to have parents' permission to include their child's number in the class directory. Each child's name is listed, in alphabetical order. Check for correct spelling. Every telephone number must be entered precisely and neatly. Due to the careful listing and copy work required, this activity may be used with a remedial group. The pupils may use carbon paper and make copies for each member of the class. A room directory of names and addresses may be made at Christmas or Valentine's Day for reference by the pupils.

361. Prepare several packs of 3″x5″ word cards, with five words to a pack. Give each player a pack of cards. At the teacher's signal, every player arranges his word cards alphabetically. The first one to complete the task correctly scores five points, the second to finish scores four points, etc.

When round one has been completed, each player passes his group of word cards to the child on his right. The cards are shuffled; then, when the signal is given, each player arranges his new group in alphabetical order.

The game continues until each player has used every group of word cards. The player with the highest score is the winner.

Sample word card groups:

    Group 1—barn   road   church   window   party
    Group 2—field   dirt   baby   lake   kitchen

362. Old telephone books may provide a unique teaching experience for children. Collect last year's directories, and make a list of names to be found in them. These names may be listed on the board or on a ditto sheet. The class looks up each name and records the code for that name. *For instance:* Smith, Robert P.: 35–3–18 (35 = page, 3 = column, 18 = number of entry in the column).

VARIATION: The teacher may supply the code and have the class look up the names and alphabetize them.

Ability to Interpret Guide Words

363. Dictionary Code. Intermediate level students enjoy codes and ciphers. Using the same dictionary that is used for class work, write a simple sentence in code on the board, or duplicate copies of several sentences that will peak their curiosity.

Example:

1	2	3
94	1	6
—	—	—
—	—	—
—	—	—
—	—	—
—	—	—

Column 1 refers to the *page* in the dictionary

Column 2 refers to the *column* on that page

Column 3 refers to *number of words* down that column

This code reads, "Who has a new baby?" (*Thorndike-Barnhart Beginning Dictionary*—Scott, Foresman).

Students could write notes to classmates in code, putting the dictionary to interesting use.

Students might volunteer to put messages on the board on their assigned days.

364. Two guide words may be written on the board. A game is played by allowing a specified amount of time and asking the students to list as many words as they can think of which would appear between these two guide words. Allow one point for each correct response; any incorrect words subtract from the score. The person with the most points wins. This game may also be used as team competition.

Ability to Interpret Pronunciation Key

365. Divide the class into teams. Provide a dictionary for each student. Write a word on the chalkboard. Signal the teams to open their dictionaries, find the word and pronounce it correctly. The first student to do so wins a point for his team.

366. Write one vowel and one word containing that vowel on the board, such as **e** in **shelf.** Students use the pronunciation key in their dictionaries to locate a word with the same vowel sound. They list as many words as they know which contain the same vowel sound. Score one point for each correct word listed. A time limit should be set. The game may continue using other vowel sounds.

367. Using the International Phonetic Alphabet in lieu of the traditional alphabet, the student writes a short story or a note to a friend. This alphabet may be found in most dictionaries.

Example:

aɪ dʒɘmt ōvɘr ʒɘ dits kæn jiᵁ?

Ability to Comprehend Definitions

368. To review guide words and alternate meanings, the child looks up a word in the dictionary. He enters the word and some of its meanings on one side of a card or paper. On the back, he writes the sentence given and then rewrites it, using synonyms for the word listed.

Example:

    acquire—gain, get
    He wanted to acquire some property.
    He wanted to get some property.
    He wanted to gain some property.

369. Dictionaries may be used to locate information about famous people. The following practice game may be used with small groups. List the names of several important people on the board. Give the students a certain amount of time, and have them look up the persons in the dictionary and find reasons why they are considered important. They may write these on paper or on the chalkboard. The pupil having the greatest number of correct answers within the time period is the winner.

Ability to Try Several Definitions in Context

370. Give students ditto sheets with several sentences on them. Be sure each sentence contains words with multiple meanings. Underline these words. Students check the dictionary to determine which number definition is used for each word. He writes the number above each one for checking purposes.

Examples:

                         2   6

The boy received a <u>letter</u> saying he had won a <u>letter</u> in football.

           16   1

The boy <u>drew</u> a picture of a dining <u>table</u>.

371. A short paragraph is written on the board or a ditto page. Several hard words should be included. Emphasis is placed on the fact that many words have more than one meaning. The hard words are located in the dictionary, and the group discusses which meaning "fits in" with the rest of the sentence.

372. Involve math, social studies or science along with a sense of fun in learning to use the dictionary.

Examples:

1. Find the combined lengths of a vole, a walrus and a newborn alligator.
2. Which is largest: crickets, centipedes or inchworms?
3. Which would you enjoy for dessert: trifle, stroganoff or mush?
4. If you were going fishing, would you take: a fly, a velocipede or a leader?
5. If you lived in Scotland, would you wear: brogans, a serape or a sporan?

373. Give each student a ditto containing several sentence groups. Each group should contain three sentences, with one word underlined in each. In two of the sentences the word has the same meaning, while in the other it has a different one. Students indicate the two sentences with the same meaning by putting a ✓ in front of them.

✓___ Mother taught me to <u>drive</u> the car.

_____ How far can you <u>drive</u> a golf ball?

✓___ Will you <u>drive</u> me to the store?

Usage Terms and Abbreviations

374. Students list as many abbreviations as they can. They may categorize them into states, streets, linear measure, days, months, time or miscellaneous abbreviations. This can help call attention to abbreviations and their correct usage.

375. To review state abbreviations, clues may be made up to remind students of certain abbreviations. The clues may be duplicated and given to each player in the group. Have the players write the correct responses and suggested abbreviations; or, two players may orally quiz each other. Each correct answer counts one point, and the player with the most points wins.

Examples of clues:

The vessel in which Noah and his family sailed.   ark   (Ark.)

Pro is for something, _____ is against.   con   (Conn.)

A medical doctor is called an _____.   MD   (Md.)

II. LIBRARY SKILLS

Table of Contents

376. Ask the children to open their books to the table of contents. Ask questions that may be answered by using the table of contents.

Examples:

"Is there a story in this book about a cowboy?

On what page does it begin?

How long is the story?

Who is the author?

Are there any poems in the book?

How do you know?"

377. Direct students to the table of contents in their English text; ask questions which can be answered from it:

"Is there a chapter about verbs?

On what page is the chapter about pronouns?

How many pages are in the chapter about pronouns?

Does the chapter about letter-writing have illustrations?"

Card Catalog

378. The children make a numbered list of books they have read. In a second column, the authors' names are listed but in mixed order. The children match each title and author by placing the number of the book in front of the author's name. They may refer to the card catalog for assistance.

379. After the children have been given explanation and training with card catalogs, give them a chance to use them. For practice, they make out index cards for given books. To give additional training, the children may be asked to catalog their classroom books, using the filing system previously learned.

380. Supply students with a number of books and five cards headed as follows: **A–E, F–J, K–O, P–T, U–Z.** They list each book on the appropriate card according to title, author's name and subject matter.

Reference Books

381. Charts showing the information to be found in reference sources should be made for all books available. Charts could be made for such sources as the encyclopedia, dictionary, Rue Subject Index or Book of Authors. After the charts have been made, questions should be asked such as:

1. To look up the meaning of **transportation,** I will use _____.
2. To look up the history of transportation, I will use _____.

382. A crossword puzzle is made using clues concerning information about mountain peaks, famous countries or rivers. Divide the group into pairs of partners, and provide reference materials such as geography books, World Almanacs and the Atlas. The teams use the reference books in completing the puzzle. Clues will pertain to the subject being studied.

Mountains:

1. Highest peak in the United States.
2. Explorer had this peak named for him.
3. Highest peak in Oregon.
4. Famous heads carved in mountain.

383. As a check on reference books and the material contained in them, list a variety of reference books in the first column, and a short description of the type of information contained in each one in a second column. The descriptive phrases should be placed in mixed order. The child is to match each reference book with its descriptive phrase by placing the number of the correct reference book in front of its description.

Examples:

    1. Who's Who in America   (3) word definitions

    2. Encyclopedia   (1) biographies of famous people

    3. Dictionary   (2) facts on many subjects

384. Divide the group into two teams. List four types of reference materials on the board: Atlas, World Almanac, Dictionary, Encyclopedia. Taking turns, ask children questions such as, "Where would you find background information on Alexander Graham Bell?" He must tell the reference material used and justify his answer. If correct, he gains one point for each part of his answer. After each player has been given a turn, the game is over. The team with the most points is the winner. Additional reference materials may be added to increase the difficulty of the game.

385. Players receive a game card such as the one below. List a category at the top of each card, and a five-letter word under it. Avoid words containing **q, y, z** or double letters. The cards may be laminated or covered with acetate, to allow answers to be written and erased. Players fill in all the blocks, using the correct categories and beginning letters. Research materials such as the Atlas, dictionary, encyclopedia or textbooks may be used to locate answers. If a player has an answer different from anyone else's, he scores five points. If two players have the same answer, each one scores three points. If three or more have the same answer, each player receives one point.

Index

386. A list of words taken from the index of a reader is listed on the board or a chart. Pupils look up each word, and write the page numbers on which information concerning this subject may be found.

Example:

    1. Cows   4. Pets

    2. Africa   5. Highways

    3. Indians

Animals	Cities	Countries	Rivers	Famous People
T	H	I	N	K
toad	Ha Giang	India	Niger	Keller
tiger	Houston	Iran	Nene	Kennedy

387. The teacher lists the material and page numbers contained in the index for a particular topic.

For example:

    Boats:

        Advantages of boat travel, 11-15

        Construction, 10-17

        Early travel, 18-19

        Various kinds of, 20-22

The children are then given questions and asked to indicate the pages where the information would appear:

        What part of the boat is called the bow?

        Name five different kinds of boats.

        When was the first large vessel launched?

388. The index of features from the daily newspaper can provide practice in locating information. If possible, each child should have a paper, or the index may be duplicated. This exercise is good for small group activities. After studying the index, questions may be asked.

Examples:

Index of Features

Amusements . . . C–10	Death Notices . . . B–4
Bridge . . . C–6	Editorials . . . A–4
Classified Ads . . . C–12-C–19	Financial . . . A–17-A–19

Bob is going to the movies. He would look in part _____, page _____.

Janet wants a job for the summer. She should check the _____ on page _____.

Tommy is learning to play bridge. He should look in part _____, page _____.

389. Each child should be furnished a city newspaper. A problem may be presented, the solution to which is to be found in the paper. The child examines the paper and locates the solution to the problem.

Example:

> 1. You are going to the show. Find a picture you want to see. Where is it playing? What time does it begin? Who is starring in the film? What is the rating?

390. Give students a list of questions based on an indexed book. Each question should contain a key word which, when located in the index, leads to information answering the question. Have students underline the key word in each question.

> In what countries are diamond mines located?
> Which colonial territory did the Lost Colony inhabit?
> What causes the changing of oceanic tides?

Projects in Finding Resource Materials for Reports

391. *Hint:* Use recordings, films, filmstrips and other related materials as listed in the manual to enrich the child's background for each unit or story. Do not neglect the search through available catalogs and lists provided by publishers.

392. A small group of children may work on a class mural. Information learned in a science, social studies, reading or health unit may be displayed in mural form. A committee may screen ideas and assign objects or space on the mural to be completed. Encourage students to use a wide variety of textured material, such as cloth, cotton, trim or wallpaper.

393. On a chart, list questions which arise in class discussions. Have the students locate information on subjects which particularly interest them. Students and the teacher may gather pictures and printed material from information sources. During small group discussions, the information, pictures and related books may be shared. The collected information may also be organized and arranged as a bulletin board display.

394. *Hint:* List several topics for research. Before the group begins, discuss possibilities of good books and key words to use for research. Make use of the library facilities to find resource materials for the report.

395. Small groups use current events to set up a news program. One student summarizes the news, making use of maps, drawings, photographs or other visual aids in his presentation. "Anchor men" report situations in foreign countries, such as floods, fighting, riots or hijackings. A different news team reports weekly.

396. A booklet may be made containing biographical information on a famous person in America (such as Lincoln, Kennedy or Eisenhower). A general outline may be set up by the teacher, giving some topic headings. The pupil researches the person, then completes the outline and writes a biography from the outline.

Chapter Seven

CONTENT READING SKILLS

Rationale

As the pupil enters the study of the content fields, his reading rapidly expands beyond the simple interpretation of story-type material. Many graphic and visual aids appear in his textbooks and demand a different approach than word-by-word or line-by-line reading. Basic reading skills make almost no contribution to handling these new media. The research on children's development of these content reading skills is not encouraging, for it indicates that many pupils cannot interpret this illustrative material.

Ideally speaking, the child would be given special instruction and help by the teacher every time she used a content textbook with a group. She would be pointing out similarities and differences among graphs, maps, charts and globes and teaching children how to read and interpret them, while they are in actual use during the lesson. But surveys of teacher practices show that this realistic approach is not common, for often the teacher has not been trained in the relevant reading techniques. She is more apt to depend upon the exercises in workbooks than on directed practice in the situations and materials present in the classroom.

BEHAVIORAL OUTCOMES

The child will learn to:

>   find cardinal and general directions on a map
>
>   locate places on maps and globes
>
>   read map symbols and keys
>
>   compare map projections
>
>   make and use charts, graphs and time lines
>
>   make and interpret simple tables

I. MAP AND GLOBE SKILLS

Ability to Orient Oneself in Relation to the Immediate Environment of the Classroom, School and Community

397. A group of children make a map of their neighborhood, community or school. Discussion should be held concerning scale and symbols. Let the children decide on a scale and appropriate symbols to use, and draw the map accordingly. Practice may be given in locating streets, buildings, parks, rivers and distances from one location to another.

398. A detailed map of the neighborhood should be made. It should include streets, parks, homes, buildings and other features. A child will be asked to tell things he would see on the way to school or to a designated store. Attention should be called to safe routes to school and other destinations. The amount of detail would vary according to the age of the child.

399. Make two outline maps of the room, showing desk locations. Each member of the class pretends to be a tree. One child is "it," and leaves the room; two other children are chosen to be "fire wardens." One pupil places a marker, representing fire, on a desk in the room. Each "fire warden" draws a line on his outline map, starting at his own location, going through the point of the fire and ending at the opposite side of the map. After each warden marks his map, the marker is removed and the child who is "it" returns. By putting the two outline maps together and finding where the lines intersect, he attempts to locate the tree on fire.

Reading a Map According to Cardinal Directions

400. A student or the teacher tells a story about someone going somewhere. Be sure the story contains several changes of directions. After the story is completed, have the students draw a diagram of how the person gets there. If desired, a simple map of the local area can be used. Blocks may be used to represent buildings near the school.

401. Have students identify "vacation spots" or other locations on a map by listing latitudes and longitudes. Each student may list latitudes and longitudes and have other students try to locate his designated area.

402. On the board, draw an intersection showing two streets. Indicate cardinal directions. Below are given directions as to stores, schools and other things located at the intersection. Have pupils read the instructions and indicate the locations according to cardinal directions.

> 1. There is a vacant lot on the NW corner. Write the word **lot** on this corner.
> 2. Filling stations are located on both the SW and SE corners. Draw squares to indicate their locations.

Finding General Directions on a Map or Globe

403. A child may be asked to tell about the most interesting place he has visited outside his own community, and how he got there. For young children, the teacher records the stories and prints them on charts for the children to read later. A community map may be used to show the route taken. The means of transportation may also be discussed. With older children, trips outside the city or state may be used and routes traced on road maps.

404. A good way to practice map skills is to plan a trip the child would like to take. By studying road maps, he marks his exact route. In order

learn to read and interpret maps and graphs, children must be trained
develop this type of reading skill. They must be taught map scales
nd symbols in order to interpret the information accurately.

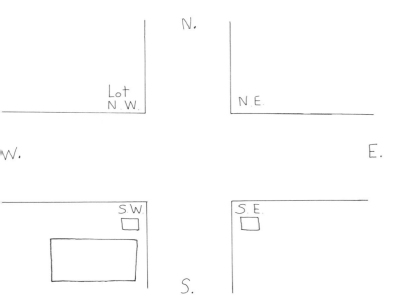

ecognizing Scale and Distance on Maps

05. After the class has been exposed to the eight main compass points,
ley draw maps of camp sites, state parks or their neighborhood. They
ake up stories, using map directions to explain the incidents involved.
ther students follow the directions to locate the places referred to in
le stories.

06. Maps, brochures and pamphlets may be glued inside folders, along
ith questions pertaining to them.

For example:

1. Find Tallahassee on the map.
2. How far is it from Jacksonville, Florida to Charleston, South
   Carolina?
3. Name the states through which the Mississippi River flows.

Locating Places on Maps and Globes

407. Various maps or outlines are given out. Have the students locate cities, rivers, products, mountains and other features, or have them color and label designated areas.

408. An outline map of an area should be given to a small group of students. Number several places on the map. List the cities, rivers, mountains and other features to which these numbers refer. Allow each pupil time to refer to other maps and globes, and have them write the correct names by the corresponding numbers. The student with the most correct answers wins.

409. Political-physical maps or globes of the world may be used to give pupils practice in locating names and places. Pupils take each letter in the alphabet and list the names of physical and political features that begin with that letter. For example, a list for the letter **A** could include Africa, Asia, Amazon River, Amsterdam or Atlas Mountains. The person who has the longest correct list at the end of the time limit is the winner.

410. Draw a large intersection on the board. Show the locations of various buildings, homes, playgrounds and other features. Under the map, list several questions which can be answered by reading the map. Have the pupils complete the questions with short word answers. Check the answers together by having pupils locate the places on the map.

       1. On which street does Mike live?
       2. Does Dick live N or S of Nancy?
       3. On which street is the church located?
       4. Who lives closest to the school?
       5. What is across the street from Mike's house?

Understanding and Expressing Relative Location of School Grounds and Community Buildings; Interpreting the Effects of Locations (such as Physical Features of the Areas, Trade Routes and Climate)

411. Collect simple layouts or maps of such places as Silver Springs, Six Gun Territory or Disneyland, and have the students make up imaginary tours to various exhibits. Familiarize students with directions, symbols and other pertinent factors.

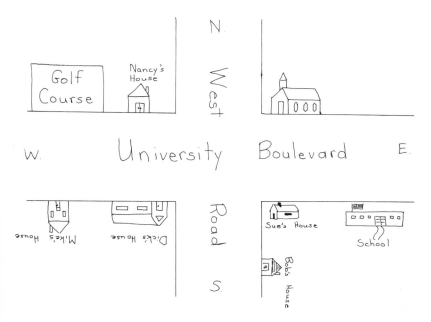

412. Furnish several maps of the local community. Small groups of students locate and mark the routes of different buses (school, city and others). A different color is used to distinguish each route. For more advanced students, symbols may be used for various stops. The pupils may become very involved in research required to mark delivery routes of local services.

Reading and Using Map Symbols, Key or Legend

413. A mural, individual drawings or a sandbox display may be used in making a community map to show areas near the school. A discussion of symbols and scales should be held, to determine the ones to be used.

414. Questions concerning the symbols, continents, oceans and other factors may be written and kept in a folder to allow for individual practice in map and globe study.

For example:

1. Which ocean is east of North America?
2. On the globe, water is represented by _____.

3. Is there more land surface or water surface on the globe?

4. Name the largest continent.

Comparing Maps and Drawing Inferences

415. *Hint:* To acquaint children with the various scales of miles used on maps, have them examine geography books, encyclopedias and loose maps. Differences in scales and symbols should be pointed out. Help students realize that maps serve various purposes. They should see and become acquainted with numerous types, not just road maps. Some to discuss are maps for weather, agriculture, climate, forest, aerial routes, navigation, solar and political maps. At the primary level, emphasis is placed on the awareness of the various kinds of maps rather than on instruction in reading them. Symbols are also necessary for map reading and understanding. The simplest ones may be illustrated on charts and discussed. Students should also become familiar with the basic map colors and what they represent—blue for water; green for forests; black for railroads and yellow for buildings.

416. Students can make a large map of their school from butcher paper. Before making a map of the school location, a walk should be taken to point out general shape and wings of classrooms, the cafeteria, the library and office facilities. Location of the school, shopping areas, streets and other familiar landmarks should be discussed.

417. Collect weather maps from newspapers. Mount these on tagboard. The teacher makes statements about a map either orally or written.

Example:

1. Children in New York must wear coats today.

2. It is cloudy somewhere in the country.

3. It is raining somewhere in the southwest.

4. It is a good day for boating on the coast.

5. A high pressure area is moving in from the east.

Students interpret the map and respond with:

1. True.

2. Not true.

3. I can't tell from the map.

II. READING GRAPHS AND CHARTS

Making, Using and Interpreting Pictorial Charts

418. To gather and retain information about people or events, students make individual charts similar to the following, or the class may make a chart as a group activity.

Famous People

Name	
Date, Place of Birth	
Family Background	
Education	
Notable Accomplishments	

419. Various books such as the *Atlas*, geography texts and the *World Almanac*, showing the population of cities in the United States, should be provided. A list of ten cities may be written on the board. Students select books, look up the cities and relist them according to population. The teacher may wish to compare the information found in each source. Other adaptations may be used to provide students with the opportunity to locate and compare information found in several different sources.

Making Circle Graphs to Show Child's Daily Program

420. After gaining sufficient knowledge of the compass and protractor, the students may make a circle graph of how they spend their time in a twenty-four–hour period. They may also make a pictorial chart.

421. After introducing the concepts of circle graphs, it would be fun for the student to make his own circle graph depicting the allotment of his time during a school day.

Note: In discussion, the students should decide which categories would be best for their particular class situation.

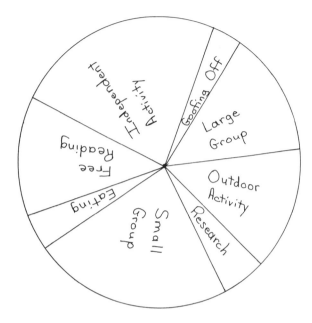

Using and Making Bar Graphs

422. In primary grades the following activity may be used to develop readiness in working with a thermometer. A thermometer graph with a movable column of "mercury" can be used to record attendance. Each day the thermometer can be changed to record the number of children present. It can also be used to record test scores or daily temperature over an extended period of time.

423. After graphs have been introduced, give students the experience of collecting data, recording it and making their own charts or graphs. Divide the class into teams. Since most children have a pet of some kind, this is a good category to use. With younger children, you may work up the basic graph together. Use categories of cats, dogs, fish, birds and other animals. Have each team appoint one person to be spokesman, one to count the responses and one to record the information on paper. Make arrangements with other classes for the teams to visit and record the information—one team to a room. The teams visit the designated rooms and inquire as to the number of pets each child has. As the questions are asked by the spokesman, the child designated counts the responses and the recorder writes the information. As each team returns to their room, they make a graph to depict the data they collected. The graphs may be displayed in the room and compared by the class.

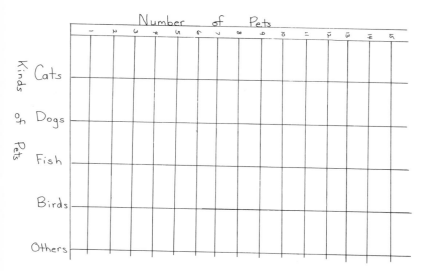

424. Each student may make a graph to show his test scores. Another exercise may be to make a chart or table showing the class average in a certain area.

425. Facts and figures are gathered by the students. They compile them to make charts and graphs to accompany reports. Students should be encouraged to draw maps or make tables to show information.

Making Time Lines to Show Chronology

426. A time line mural may be made outlining events in social studies or science development.

Examples:

1. Growth record of seeds or plants
2. Growth of communication (pony express to Telstar)
3. Designs of automobiles
4. Aviation (balloons to rockets)

427. Following the reading of a story or a book containing events that occur over an extended period of time, students will benefit from making a time line involving the events in the order of their occurrence. This may be done with printed material telling the events and dates, accompanied by student illustrations or cutouts from commercial sources.

III. READING TABLES

Interpreting and Making Simple Tables from Common Sources

428. *Hint:* The *World Almanac* is a classroom essential. It includes tables of virtually every description and category. Activities in this area may center around locating and interpreting information on population, consumption of goods, imports and exports and other categories.

429. A timetable may be made from tagboard. Students record the time and stops involved in getting to and from school or other places in the community. After reading information concerning travel abroad, the timetable may show departure and arrival schedules for trains, buses or planes.

430. Problem solving experiences should be given to enable students to use the timetables of airlines or railways. The Almanac or encyclopedia may be used for reference. A child planning an actual trip may provide just the incentive needed to create interest. Help plan the time of departure, length of the trip and time of arrival by consulting the timetable. Information may also be gathered about the city to be visited.

431. Children choose ten stocks from the New York Stock Exchange and keep a table of their daily progress.

Chapter Eight

COMPREHENSION AND INTERPRETATION SKILLS

Rationale

Some writers give us long lists of comprehension skills, despite their complete inability to demonstrate real differences among these various skills. There are only three or four recognized components of comprehension that research can find. One of these, of course, is the difficulty of the vocabulary for the reader. This component we attempt to strengthen by training in using word analysis and contextual clues. A second major component is the recognition of relationships among ideas, as in adding them together to find a main idea, distinguishing among major and minor details, following a sequence of related directions and adding ideas together to obtain an inference or conclusion. Most other so-called comprehension skills are simply extensions of these basic behaviors.

As the pupil progresses to more difficult materials, his organizing skills and rates of reading begin to influence his comprehension. He must learn to summarize and outline, to separate fact from opinion, and to vary his reading rate in different reading tasks, if he is to obtain the breadth and depth of comprehension demanded in later school life.

BEHAVIORAL OUTCOMES

The child will learn to:

> express the main idea of a given selection
>
> find and remember various details
>
> follow sequential directions
>
> coalesce ideas to draw conclusions
>
> demonstrate his comprehension in a variety of ways
>
> manipulate his rate according to his purpose and the difficulty of the material
>
> prepare simple summaries and outlines
>
> deal with materials incorporating both fact and fiction, time and cause-effect relationships

I. UNDERSTANDING WHAT IS READ

Selecting Title for Story

432. *Hint:* Always stress the main idea when selecting a title.

433. After reading a short paragraph, pupils choose the best title from a list of several possible ones, or make up original titles.

434. Have students read selected paragraphs. They must supply three titles for each one. One should be an action title, one a mood title and one a suspense title.

Locating and Remembering Details and Facts

435. *Hint:* When asking questions concerning details and facts, ask only for interesting or important information. Avoid questions that do not add to the comprehension of the selection.

436. Sentences taken from the reading assignment are written on the board or on a chart. The students read the assignment and then answer such questions as **Who, What, Where, Why, How many** and **When.**

Example:

At seven o'clock Margo and Tommy left to go to town.

      Who? _____

      When? _____

      Where? _____

437. The teacher makes phrase cards for each child based on a story previously read. She writes a question on the board which can be answered by one of the phrases. The child having the correct phrase card to answer the question, raises his hand. He reads the question from the board and the phrase card he is holding. If correct, the teacher writes the answer alongside the question.

Example:

      Where did the boys run?

      (*Answer*) Into the yard.

438. The child should read the story, then answer the questions asked about it.

THE APPLE

      The apple is red and shiny.

      It grew on a tree. The apple

      is juicy and good to eat.

QUESTIONS

1. What color is the apple?

2. Do people eat apples?

3. Do apples grow on vines?

4. What makes an apple shiny?

439. The child who is "It" says to the class, "I am thinking of the name of a country; what is it?" Students then try to guess the country by asking pertinent questions, which the one who is "It" can answer with only "Yes" or "No," such as: "Is it on the continent of Europe?"

"Is it in the southern part of Europe?" "Is it bordered by the Mediterranean Sea?" "Is it Italy?"

The one who guesses the name of the country is then "It," and the game continues with the class asking him leading questions about the country (or invention, famous person or other topic) of which he is thinking.

This game may be played by younger children by using rhyming words in this manner: the one who is "It" says, "I am thinking of a word that sounds like **cat,** and it is something to wear." The children then guess what it is, knowing that the answer must rhyme with **cat.**

440. To point up the importance of careful reading, a question or problem is written on the board. Time is allowed for the children to read it. It is then erased and detailed questions are asked concerning it. This exercise may be done using various subject matter, such as Math or Social Studies.

Example:

Tom went to the store to buy some bread. He spent 35¢ for bread and 10¢ for a candy bar. How much money did he have left?

1. What were you asked to find?
   a) How much he spent?
   b) The price of the bread?
   c) How much he had left?

2. How much did he spend?
   a) 25¢   c) 35¢
   b) 10¢   d) None of these

441. Make a set of anagrams by cutting oaktag into squares. Print one letter on each square. To have sufficient letters to form words, make thirty-six cards for each vowel and common consonants such as **h, s, t, r** and **y.** Eighteen **g**'s and **z**'s are sufficient, and twenty-four each of the remaining letters in the alphabet. After the teacher reads or assigns a short paragraph, she lists several questions about the selection. The child forms the answers by using the letters from the anagram set. One-word answers are acceptable. This type of exercise is best used with a small group.

442. After learning about various cities, the following game may be played. Several questions are made up concerning each city. A ticket agent is selected to represent each city. Before a child may board the train or boat to leave a city, he must answer the designated questions concerning that city.

443. Two different areas of information are given: A) the page numbers and paragraphs where the information can be located, and B) a sentence containing the main idea of each paragraph. The students match column A with column B. This may be used on a ditto or copied from the board.

Example:

A

a. page 134: Paragraph 2
b. page 302: Paragraph 1
c. page 309: Paragraph 4

B

1. Washington was appointed a public surveyor.
2. In 1774 he was a member of the First Continental Congress.
3. Washington was elected the first president of the United States.

444. Divide the group into two teams. Let each player have a book on his desk. The teacher asks a question that may be answered from the book. The first child who answers the question correctly wins a point for his team; the team with the most points wins. Questions may be asked about content, number of capitals, periods, vowels, sentences and other points.

Note: This activity could be related to any skill involved in reading. Tailor your questions to fit the particular skills you are stressing.

445. A fun way to check comprehension of an assigned story or unit of study, is a "Circle Review" game. The group forms a circle, and the first player asks the player on his right a question about the story or unit. If the player answers correctly, he gets a point and is the next person to ask a question. If he is not able to answer correctly, the question continues around the circle until someone answers correctly. The game continues until each person is given several chances to participate. Individual scores may be kept to see who is the winner.

Following Written Directions

446. A child or the teacher may perform several acts, such as raising a hand, opening a drawer, lifting an eraser and drawing a line on the board. The children are asked to write the acts in the order in which they were performed.

447. To carry out an activity or experiment, the teacher lists specific directions on the board. The children listen to them or silently read the directions and carry them out.

Example:

HOW TO MAKE BUTTER
1. Pour a small amount of heavy cream into a baby food jar.
2. Tightly seal the jar.
3. Shake until a ball of butter forms in the jar.
4. Drain the excess liquid.
5. Add salt.
6. Spread on a cracker and EAT!

448. Let each child in the group write a series of directions for acts that can be performed in sequence in the room. Let one child read five of his directions; have another child listen and then try to perform them in proper sequence.

For example:

1. Stand up and face the back of the room.
2. Erase the back board.
3. Open and close the door.
4. Carry a library book to the teacher.
5. Return to your desk and be seated.

449. Using strips of tagboard showing action directions, each child pulls a strip from the stack. He reads the strip and follows the directions. This may be used as a dismissal activity.

Examples:

1. Stand on one foot.
2. Write your name on the board.
3. Turn around three times.
4. Find a piece of paper bigger than a book.
5. Find a black shoe.

450. Assemble stories in acetate covers. Several written questions are listed at the bottom or on back of the page. The child reads the story, then follows the given directions.

(story)

1. Draw a line under the phrase that tells what Virginia found on the table.
2. Circle all names in the story.
3. Draw a picture to show the surprise Virginia had.

451. Give students a sheet of paper with numerals in the positions shown below. On the board, print written directions as follows:

1. Connect numerals 2, 4 and 8 with a straight line.
2. Connect 5, 8, 6 and 9 with straight lines.
3. Draw squares around each of the following numerals: 1, 3, 9.

1	2	3
4	5	6
7	8	9

452. On the board or on a ditto sheet, print several letters of the alphabet, four across and four down, leaving space in between. Written directions should accompany them.

For example:

1. Draw a square around the letter **C.**
2. Form a triangle by connecting **D, G** and **X.**
3. Starting with **M,** use a broken line (--------) and connect **M** and **S.**
4. Draw a straight line from **L** to **O,** passing through **R.**
5. Circle all letters which are vowels.

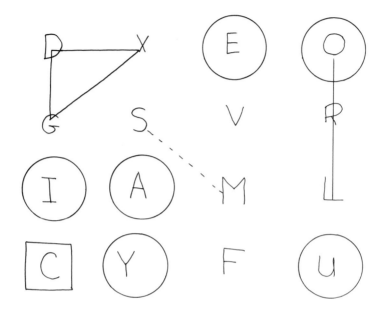

453. Give students a piece of paper showing dots in the positions as shown opposite.

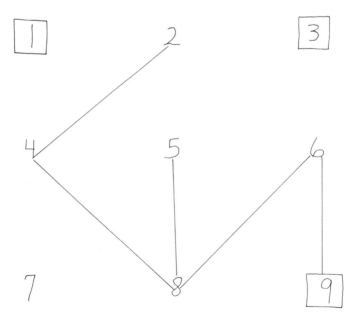

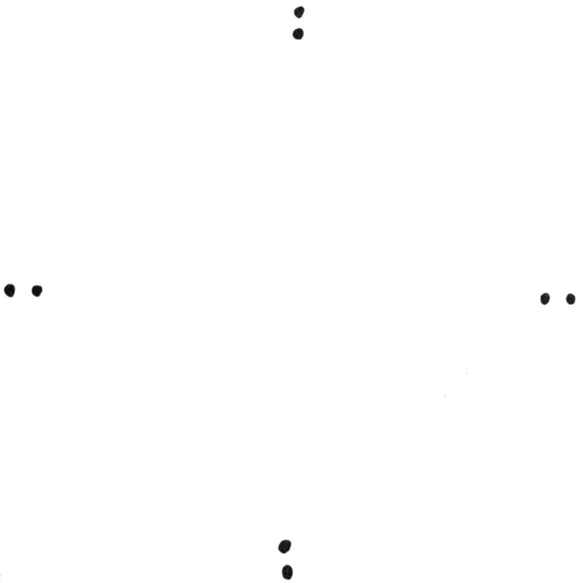

•
•

• •   • •

•
•

On the board or chart, print written directions as follows:

1. Make a large square, using the dots as a guide.
2. Within the large square, draw a circle touching the square on all four sides.
3. Within the circle, draw another square, touching the circle at four points.
4. With your crayon, shade the area outside the inner square and within the inner circle.
5. Within the last square, draw any geometric shape or shapes you wish. Be sure the shape touches the square at three or four points.

454. The class plans an activity together. Children are assigned specific jobs, and their duties are listed on the board. The children must refer to the board for directions concerning their jobs.

For example:

Jane and Sue will clear the work counter.

Tom, Henry and Sam will move the desks to the sides of the room.

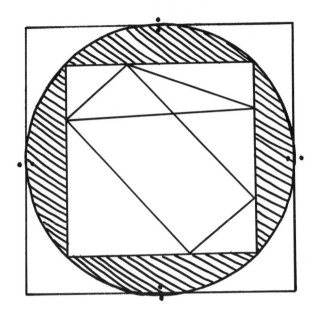

455. List several sentences on the board. Some should call for listening for comprehension, and some for following written directions. Have students read the sentences and give the correct responses.

Example:

1. In the top right-hand corner of your paper, write your name and grade.

2. Draw five kittens. Color four brown and one black.

3. Draw a circle around the black kitten.

4. There are three girls in the front row. Write the name of the girl who has blond hair.

Drawing Conclusions

456. To develop sentence understanding, a teacher will ask various types of questions. Be sure to ask questions involving critical thinking as well as factual recall.

Example:

> The leaves were falling from the trees. Tom and Mary were playing nearby. Dad came outside with a rake and began to pick up the different colored leaves. Tom and Mary ran over to help. What did Dad bring outside? What was the season?

457. Using a reading text or other subject matter textbook, have the students locate sentences on a given page that tell **How, When, Where, Why** or **Who.**

458. Direct the class to read a story from the text which contains an illustration. Have students point out sentences that refer specifically to the picture; then, have them point out sentences containing information which could *not* be learned by looking at the picture.

459. A short paragraph may be duplicated or written on the board for each child to read. Various phrases from the paragraph are written over, in two separate columns. The child draws a line to connect the two parts of each sentence. This exercise may be duplicated or used with the overhead projector as a small group activity.

Example:

> Mary and Bill went to the store. Each had ten cents to spend. Mary bought a candy bar and Bill got a kite.

Mary and Bill went	kite
Bill bought a	candy
Mary spent ten cents on	to the store

460. At the top of a ditto sheet or on the board, draw four or five toys and indicate a price beside each one. Below the pictures, print questions about the toys which may be answered either by filling in a numerical answer or by putting "Yes" or "No" in the blank. Pupils read the sentences and complete the blanks.

461. Ditto sentences pertaining to five objects. After each sentence, write a number for the position of the described object. Leave a blank space at the top of the paper. Have students read each sentence and draw a descriptive illustration in the given position.

462. On a transparency, write the words **who, what, when, where** and **how**—each in a different color of ink. Below these words, write such phrases as "Frank and his dog"; "quickly and quietly"; "the moon"; "on the playground"; "during the game."

Read each phrase aloud and have the class determine which of the five questions it answers.

FOLLOW-UP: Give the class duplicated copies of certain sentences and have them underline, at the teacher's direction, the word or phrase in each sentence which answers one of the five basic questions.

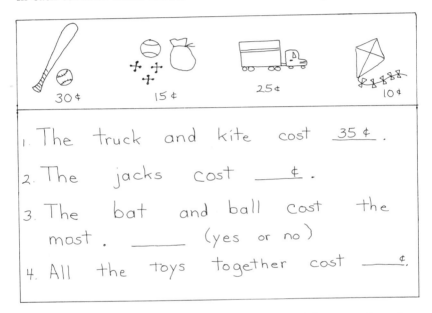

463. After the group has completed a book containing several stories, divide them into two teams. Questions or statements may be written on the board or asked orally, to see which team can locate the answers and accumulate the most points.

Example:

    1. In which story did the train wreck occur?

    2. There was a terrible thunderstorm.

464. After children read an assigned text, questions such as the following may be written on charts:

    1. List two reasons for the quarrel.

    2. Why did Mr. Smith act the way he did?

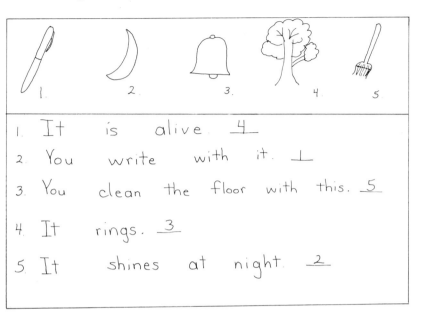

1. It is alive. __4__
2. You write with it. __1__
3. You clean the floor with this. __5__
4. It rings. __3__
5. It shines at night. __2__

465. Write several brief stories. Duplicate them or enclose them in acetate. Skill exercises accompany each paragraph. Some may require multiple-choice answers, while others may contain words to be underlined or circled. The children are allowed a short time to read each paragraph and complete the exercise.

Example:

> A large crowd was gathering around the pool. The meet was about to begin. As the whistle sounded, the swimmers dived into the water. The race was very close. The crowd watched with mounting excitement. The boy in lane two was edging his way up on the leader in lane four. As the leader lunged forward in a final effort, he touched the wall only seconds before his opponent. The crowd cheered and shouted with excitement.
>
> The winner was:
> __X__ in lane four
> __ in lane two
> __ in lane five

466. The children are given a mimeographed sheet containing a short story and a diagram. Questions are written on the left side of the diagram, and the children complete the answers on the right side.

Example:

The Taylors had left their home in Jacksonville and were moving to the mountains. They traveled many hours before arriving. Tommy was very excited. He had heard about his new home but he couldn't wait to see it for himself. He nearly leaped from the car and bounded up the winding stairs. He knew exactly which room was his and where things would be kept. Under the wide windows, Dad was building a long row of cabinets. This would be a perfect place for his games and sports equipment. After looking things over carefully, he remembered the car still had to be unloaded. He hurried downstairs to help.

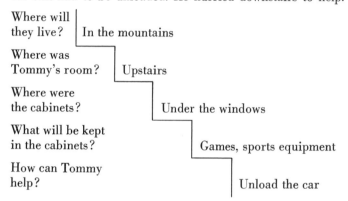

Where will
they live?   In the mountains

Where was
Tommy's room?   Upstairs

Where were
the cabinets?   Under the windows

What will be kept
in the cabinets?   Games, sports equipment

How can Tommy
help?   Unload the car

467. Direct each student to read a story about a famous person (invention, event in history, nation); then, have him write down ten clues as to the person's identity. The clues should become progressively more explicit, without revealing the person's identity. Select one student to read his first clue; then have the class guess the person's identity. If they are unable to do so with the first clue, have the student read the second, third and so on, until one student guesses the person's name. The one who guesses correctly then proceeds to read his clues, again one clue at a time.

II. INTERPRETATION THROUGH SHARING

Dramatization

468. Have children choose roles and read or dramatize the conversation between characters, stressing the need to "talk like real people," "show how you feel by your voice" and other such factors.

469. Give each student a duplicate book. One child silently acts out part of a story previously read. The first person to locate that part of the story reads it orally.

470. This is an activity for two or more players. The child who is "It" selects a news item from a page of the newspaper and proceeds to act it out. The others look at the page and try to guess the item to which he is referring.

471. Allow students to perform certain actions described in the text, such as "sauntering about," "swaggering" or "loping along." Urge them to show by their own actions and expressions how the character looked and acted.

472. Dramatizations of scenes from stories with which the class is not familiar may encourage other students to read the stories. The productions may be elaborate, with stage settings and costumes, or they may be simple, with little preparation.

The actors may construct their own narration and dialogue, or they may learn excerpts from the author's words.

473. While the children are reading an unfamiliar story, have them stop at a dramatic or interesting episode. Instruct them to cover the next few lines with paper and try to anticipate what will happen next. Urge the students to use both illustrations and text in deciding the probable ensuing action.

474. Write on the chalkboard words for emotions, such as **happiness, fear, anger** and **love.** The children dramatize each of them, using various facial expressions, gestures and tones of voice.

FOLLOW-UP: To further develop the ability to empathize, have the class dramatize a familiar story. Prepare them for the portrayal by first discussing the plot, characters and setting, and the most effective techniques of achieving tone and emotional reaction.

475. For practice in oral reading and communication, pupils may write a radio script using such topics as "Modern Space Travel" or "Weather Satellites" and produce it on a tape recorder. Advanced students may want to carry this activity a step further, and expand it into a "live television" presentation.

476. Students may use a story from a reader or a library book to simulate a radio play. Give special attention to sound effects.

Art Activities

477. Divide the board into four squares. In each square, write a sentence which is to be illustrated. Have the class fold their paper into four sections, write the sentences and illustrate them as accurately as possible.

> The clown has a peanut on his nose.
> Follow a rabbit with a long trunk.
> See the girl with a lion on a string.
> I can make a fancy kite.

Students will enjoy looking for descriptive phrases in their books which they can illustrate.

The clown has a peanut on his nose.	A rabbit with a long trunk.
A girl with a lion on a string.	A fancy kite.

478. Flannel board characters and scenes provide an interesting way of presenting a book. Students may make the figures from felt or draw them on heavy paper. If paper figures are used, glue a small piece of sandpaper, felt or pellon on the back of each one so it will stick to the flannel. Each child may narrate his own story as he displays the scenes.

479. Children will enjoy making hand or stick puppet characters taken from a story. These may then be used to dramatize the story for others.

480. Students may use clay to mold characters taken from a story. These may be used for stimulation in discussing character analysis or in a review of the story.

481. Arrange on the bulletin board a series of bordered sheets of paper. Head each paper with a method of reporting or sharing a book. Students sign the sheets, indicating their choices. Change headings often as students think of different ways to share books.

Examples:

> Puppetry, diorama, character analysis, drawing, skit, written report.

482. The title of a book and its characters may be displayed by using simple mobiles made from clothes hangers.

483. On the board or on a chart, print a short paragraph about a descriptive scene. Have students read the paragraph carefully and illustrate what it tells.

Example:

> Bob was outside, playing catch with two of his friends. His sister Sue was playing Jacks with Milly. Three other boys were wading in the puddle by the edge of the road. Mother and Aunt Ruth were sitting in the yard, watching the children at play. The sun was beginning to come out from behind the gray clouds and a beautiful rainbow was visible behind the treetops.

484. A book diorama is an activity which can be undertaken by the class as a group or by individuals.

The class (or individual) selects a scene from a book and reconstructs it inside a box from which the top has been removed. The box may be decorated appropriately, using construction paper, paints or other media, and the characters may be made from cardboard or clay.

485. After a story or book has been read, a discussion may follow to call attention to materials mentioned in the story. Students may then describe or make objects they could construct from the materials mentioned.

For example: If wood were mentioned, students could construct a house, a table, a boat or a shelf.

486. A Unique Way of Reviewing a Book. Use the format of comic strips. Give students a long piece of drawing paper. They divide it into boxes. Each box is filled in with sequence scenes of the story. Print the title and author along the top of the strip. If they wish, the children may write a short summary of the story on the back of the strip.

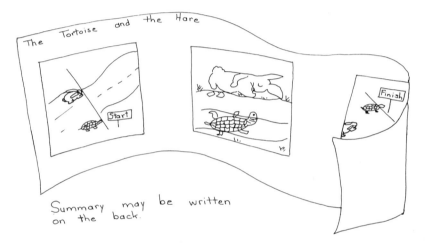

487. Book covers often create interest in a book by their colors, or by the designs, moods or adventures they depict. Students can show their interest in books by making creative book jackets. *Remember:* a book jacket tells three major things: the title, the author and an interesting picture about the story. Later, students may want to write their own stories to staple inside the jackets. These books may be placed on the reading table for all the class to enjoy.

Book Reviews

488. Book jackets may be displayed on library tables or bulletin boards to create interest. The titles and authors are discussed, and children are asked to share other stories written by the same author.

489. Have students select a library book of their choice. They may share something about the book, describe the main characters or read an interesting portion of it to a small group.

490. Comprehension may be strengthened by having children read a paragraph then answer questions according to given directions. One publication offering exercises of this type is the *Gates-Peardon Practice Exercises in Reading, Type C* (Bureau of Publication, Teachers College, Columbia University, New York).

Example:

> After reading a specific play, ask the following questions:
> 1. List in order the directions given for producing *Rumpelstiltskin* as a play.
>   1.
>   2.
>   3.
> 2. Underline the correct choice: The directions indicate that Rumpelstiltskin should be played by (a boy), (a girl), (an old man).
> 3. The requirements call for _____ scenes or _____ stage sets to produce the play.
> 4. The directions specify three special 'props.' They are as follows:
>   1.
>   2.
>   3.

491. To share reading experiences, children may make bulletin board book reviews. After the student has read a book, he writes on a 3″x5″ card such information as title, author, setting, a one- or two-sentence plot summary and a brief explanation of why he liked the book. The cards are to be tacked to the bulletin board for others to read.

VARIATION: File the cards in a file box to be kept on the library table.

Character Analysis

492. After reading a story to the class, lead them in a review of the plot and of the characters' responses to each situation. Urge pupils to cite evidences in the story of each character's mood and manner. Then, have certain students read the conversations again, capturing the character's reactions by tone and emphasis.

493. Give each child a duplicated copy of a brief story which contains a spirited dialogue (or refer to a passage in the text). Instruct the class to skim the selection to find words and phrases used instead of the word **said,** to give a more definite description of how the characters felt and sounded. As they find such phrases as **whispered Bill, he stammered, agreed Eric** or **David remarked,** have them read the passages aloud and describe the character's emotional intent.

FOLLOW-UP: As a writing experience, students may compose one-paragraph conversations, substituting descriptive words or phrases for the word **said.**

494. Read, without inflection, dramatic excerpts of conversation from a familiar story. Ask the class whether the characters would have spoken differently—and if so, how and why. Then, have children read the dialogue, using stress and tone of voice to show how the characters felt when they spoke.

495. After the class has read a story, write on the chalkboard words and phrases which describe the emotional responses of the characters. Have students name the character who experienced each response, and describe the events in the story which evoked the particular emotion.

496. Questions such as the following may accompany an assigned reading.

Example:

>Why do you think John acted as he did (page 45, line 8)?
>
>What did the author mean by the sentence on page 89, line 2?

497. The characters in literature lend themselves to identification and emotional understanding. Less emphasis is placed on the children's organization of facts, and more on their emotional involvement with the characters. After reading a paragraph describing a story character, the students may be asked several questions requiring critical thinking and character judgments.

Example:

>She was exquisitely dressed in a famous creation, her fur draped over her shoulder. Her hair was impeccably neat and her eyes twinkled as she looked over the waves of blooming flowers. Her skin was clear and free of wrinkles. She seemed happy and content, looking at the beautiful flowers.

1. What kind of person do you think she is?
2. Where do you think she lives?
3. Is she poor?
4. What kind of things do you think she likes other than flowers?

498. To organize information about story characters, students may locate and read aloud the answers to questions such as these:

Who is the main character?
What does he look like?
Where does he live?
What does he like to do?
How does he act?

499. After the students have read a story containing a particular character, they may write an analysis of him. The sketch may pertain only to information found in the story, or it may include personal impressions of the character which were not described in the story.

III. RATE IMPROVEMENT

Speed

500. *Hint:* For reinforcement of learning, children should be given the opportunity to read a great deal of material at least one grade below their reading level. The content should be checked to be sure it corresponds to their age and interest level. This reinforcement will help develop and improve their rate of reading.

501. Speed of reading is effective only when the child comprehends what he reads. Word recognition and comprehension are necessary to ensure speed. A child may be able to read grade level material but still possess a slow reading rate. If this is true, emphasis should be placed on speed while retaining comprehension. To enable a child to keep track of his own progress, a chart may be kept recording the results of the timed readings.

The reading rate of children may be checked with a small group. Be sure the material is at the proper grade level and new to the children. Have them read rapidly but carefully enough to comprehend the material. For grades four and above, three- or four-minute tests may be used. Short comprehension checks should also be made.

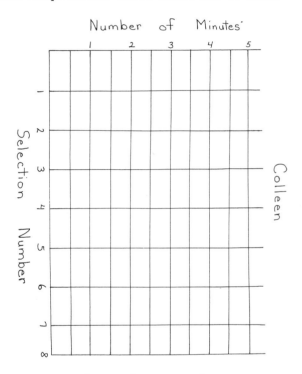

502. To increase speed in reading, many devices may be used. Flash cards bearing words and phrases of increasing lengths, as well as paragraphs with comprehension questions (with a timing device and emphasis on increasing one's reading rate), are some types often used. Always keep an adequate supply of material available that isn't too difficult for the group.

Skimming and Scanning

503. Discuss with the class the fact that newspapers are designed for quick and easy reading—skimming. The first sentence of an article usually answers four basic questions (**who, what, when, where**), and the remainder of the article adds the details.

Instruct each student to bring a newspaper article to class. Have several students place their articles in an opaque projector, so that the class can determine the answers to the four basic questions.

504. The newspaper is a good source for speeding up reading. Give a child a page from the paper, and ask him to skim the content for about two minutes. When the time is up, have him fold the page and list as many different topics as he can recall from the page. A record may be kept to compare his progress over various intervals of time.

505. Instruct the class to read a passage from their text, finding as quickly as possible the answer to a specific question, such as: "Find the names of the two main exports of Canada." Allow more time in the beginning for scanning, but shorten the time as the students become more proficient.

506. Upper grade children will enjoy this news activity. Choose five news categories (local politics, national politics, sports, theatre, science), and five prominent people associated with each area. A bar graph or table is kept to show how often each person's name is mentioned daily in the newspaper.

IV. ORGANIZING SKILLS

Separating Fact from Fiction (Exaggerations)

507. Phrases taken from story books may be listed on the board. The children circle all statements which are fiction or which cannot be seen on earth.

1. a lady flying with an umbrella
2. a cow jumping over the moon
3. an elephant talking
4. two cars tied together
5. a boy standing on a man's shoulders

508. Cut advertisement slogans from magazines and let pupils analyze them for a language arts lesson. Discuss whether the statements are true, a play on words, exaggerated or completely imaginative. Give each student a slogan, and have him rewrite it in a different style from its original form.

For example: If it were written as a play on words, the student could rewrite it as completely imaginative or as a truthful statement.

509. Read "tall tales" to the class, and have children listen for exaggerations and tell how many they can remember. After several tales have been read together (such as some of the Paul Bunyan stories), divide the class into groups of five or six. Let them make up a "tall tale" of a cumulative type. One child begins, and the others add to it in turn. The audience may enjoy retelling the story in sequence.

Finding Irrelevant Parts, Sorting Related Statements

510. Tell a simple story to the group. Deliberately include several irrelevant sentences. Ask the students to repeat as many of the irrelevant sentences as they can remember.

511. After reading an article expressing two different points of view, the child arranges the facts included according to each supporter's point of view.

Example:

An article on the pros and cons of smoking may be arranged as such.
1. State three harmful effects attributed to smoking.
   1.
   2.
   3.
2. State reasons why people do not want to quit smoking.
   1.
   2.
   3.

512. Give careless readers a paragraph containing various words which do not fit the meaning of the rest of the paragraph. When the child locates an incorrect word, he crosses it out and inserts a better word in its place.

> *Example:* A paragraph about pioneer days may read as follows:
> The Reed family lived in the settlement of Boonesboro. Early one evening Tom and Joe were doing their homework. They were sitting on a stool by the fireplace. The TV was going but they weren't watching. Suddenly the lights went out. Dad went to check and found a fuse had blown out. He replaced it and the electricity came back on. The boys quickly finished their homework and started watching the football game with their father.

513. Pictures of various types of communication devices are placed on the chalk tray. Each player takes his turn making statements about one of the means of sending and receiving messages. He reads them orally to the group, and they guess to which forms of communication the statements are related.

Organization of Paragraph—Topic and Summary Sentences

514. Newspaper articles and magazines may be used to study summaries. Have the students locate the main ideas in paragraphs they read.

515. Divide the group into two teams. Have one team take notes on a short talk, while the other team listens for good speech habits in delivery. When the talk is completed, have the teams compare reactions to determine if the talk was effective and interesting as well as informative. Give each student a chance to present a talk for the others. Be sure that any criticism is constructive and will help improve oral speaking habits.

516. An article discussing a controversial issue relating to social or civic affairs, a new book or a new movie may be assigned. Before reading the article, the teacher may present the author's opinion or point of view. After the children read the article, they list the author's reasons for his expressed views. With sufficient practice, the child will be able to determine the main idea and supporting facts independently.

517. Selections from newspapers, magazines or folders are read. These are consumable materials, so students may underline the main idea in red and the supporting details in blue.

VARIATION: Using the above directions, students may illustrate (draw) the main ideas and use smaller paper to illustrate supporting details. These materials and drawings may be displayed in the classroom.

518. Assign students to watch a sketch from their favorite TV variety show. Afterward, they describe the main idea and write several supporting sentences.

519. To obtain a variety of facts concerning a particular incident, have the pupil read three or four authorities' views on a subject. This activity is excellent to use with history, civics or current events. Informal debates may be held with small groups to stimulate motivation.

520. For practice in finding the main idea, write on the chalkboard:

> "Locate these selections, and write the main idea of each one in a complete sentence:
>
> page 37, paragraph 4
> page 41, paragraph 1
> page 43, paragraph 3"

521. Have students listen and take notes on newscasts. They should listen to current events reports in order to note the development of ideas from topic sentences.

Time, Cause–Effect

522. To stress the concept of cause and effect, children may be given a paragraph to read. Specific questions are asked to show cause and effect:

> Mary woke up with a sore throat. She felt very bad.
> How did Mary feel? Why?

523. After reading a paragraph, the student is given several possible answers to a question about the cause of a particular action.

Example:

> Sally and Jan went to the store to get a loaf of bread. When they arrived at the store they saw Sue, a friend of theirs. They talked for some time. Sue invited them to her house. They left with Sue without getting their bread.

The question may be:

Why did they leave without buying the bread?
    a. the store was out of bread
    b. they bought rolls instead
    c. they forgot

524. On a transparency, write twelve pairs of statements; one of each pair should state a cause, and the other, the effect.

Divide the class into two teams, and instruct them to take turns writing (with a felt-tip pen) a **C** before each cause statement and an **E** before each effect statement. One point is awarded for each pair of statements correctly identified.

Sample statements:

E	1.	We quickly rowed the boat to shore.
C	2.	A thunderstorm suddenly broke over the bay.
C	1.	The movie is over.
E	2.	People are leaving the theater.

FOLLOW-UP: Give each child a duplicated copy of sentences grouped in sets of three. Instruct the students to write **C** and **E** before the appropriate statements, ignoring the unnecessary or irrelevant statements.

525. To make community history more meaningful and interesting, let students interview older members of the community to learn facts concerning its early settlement, industry, homes and development. Invite members of the community to the classroom as resource visitors. The class may write articles or stories based on the information learned.

Sequence of Events

526. To show the sequence of a story or events of a field trip, children may display pictures, drawings and notes on an accordion chart.

527. Read a story to the class and then cite a particular incident from it. Have students describe what happened just before and just after the incident. Then, direct the class's attention to a particular illustration in the story; have them describe what event the illustration refers to, what action preceded it and what followed.

528. Put a batch of sentences in an envelope, and a story on the front of the envelope. After the child reads the story on the front, ask him to turn the envelope over and see if he can arrange the sentence strips in their correct sequence.

529. After reading a paragraph or story, the children are given a list of events to place in proper sequence as they occurred in the paragraph. To help children follow the sequence, specific questions may be asked. This activity may also be done before the story is completed, and children can try to predict the ending.

530. After reading a short paragraph, the children complete blanks or answer questions concerning the sequence of events in the paragraph.

Example:

Sam was walking down the street carrying a bag of eggs. He tripped over a stick in his path and fell. When he got up the eggs were broken.

The first event was _____.
The second event was _____.

Or, questions such as:

What happened first?
What occurred next?

531. A story is cut into paragraphs and mounted on cardboard. Each paragraph is marked so that the child may use a key to check his work. After reading the paragraphs, the child arranges them in proper sequence. This is an excellent independent activity.

532. List a variety of statements in mixed order. The children are to rearrange them in their correct sequence.

Example:

a. Harvest the corn.
b. Purchase corn from the market.

    c. Till the soil.

    d. Deliver corn to the market.

    e. Plant the seeds.

533. After listening to a story, the children are given a list of several sentences pertaining to it. They number the sentences in proper sequence as they occurred.

534. To develop awareness of the sequence of events in a story, have the class review the order of the plot, using such words as **to begin with, then, following, next, after that** and **in conclusion.** Instruct the students to examine the story for words and phrases that indicate such things as time, when an event took place or how long something lasted.

535. A "Dial and Read" chart may be made from a large rectangle. Attach a circle in the middle with a brad. Number around the circle from one to six. On both sides of the circle, place three pockets; number these from one to six also. Use six different stories, and divide each one into phrases. Place the phrase cards in different pockets. The child will spin the dial on the circle and locate the pocket with the corresponding number on which the dial lands. He draws a phrase strip from the pocket and reads it. If he can correctly read it, he may keep it; if not, he must return it to the pocket. The game continues until one child can arrange his phrase strips into a complete story.

536. A recorded story, news event or short talk is presented to the class. Have the students write the main events in correct sequence as they occurred. Reread or replay the record so the students may check their skill.

537. To aid the children in following the sequence of events in a story, a map may be made to show each event as it occurs. Have a student chart each relationship and step as it is developed in the story.

538. Students may become familiar with the legends and developments in the story of flight by using pictures, models, films, filmstrips, reference books and other source materials. Each child may draw an illustration about each stage and write a short explanation of it. The illustrations may be mounted on cardboard or projected on a screen by means of an opaque projector. Each child may read his story as his picture is shared with the group. This could be done as an oral presentation or made into a display, with the stories compiled in book form.

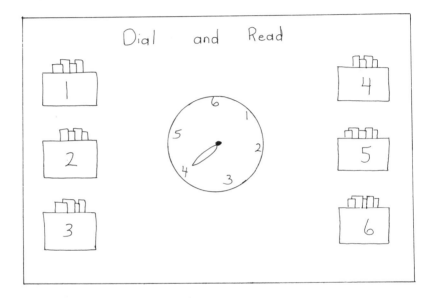

Writing Brief Summaries (Stories or Paragraphs)

539. List several short paragraphs on the board or on charts. Have the students summarize each paragraph with a single sentence.

540. Each player writes a description of a country he chooses. He tells as many facts as possible without giving the name of the country. He reads his description orally, and the other players try to guess the country. The person who guesses correctly scores one point. The player with the most points is the winner. This game may also be played with cities, the names of important people or famous landmarks.

Outlining

541. Make a simple outline form from oaktag to accompany a short selection. On the oaktag, print specific phrases needed to complete the outline. The outline phrases and frame may be kept in a large envelope. A smaller envelope containing an answer key may be attached. Students read the story, construct the outline and check their own work.

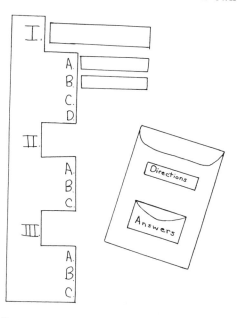

542. After reading an assigned selection, an outline may be used to organize information and ideas.

Example:

THE POLICEMAN AT WORK (pp. 25-39)

    A. Equipment used by the policeman.
       1.
       2.
       3.
       4.

    B. The jobs of a policeman.
       1.
       2.
       3.
       4.

543. Students may be given a list of words and an outline. They are to organize the words and fill in the blanks in the outline.

Example:

	I. Clothing
cabbage	A.
hat	B.
dog	C.
bird	II. Food
string beans	A.
dress	B.
shirt	C.
rabbit	III. Pets
corn	A.
	B.
	C.

544. After reading an assigned lesson, the teacher places an outline on the board and the children fill in the blanks.

Example:

ESKIMOS

I. Homes	III. Food
A.	A.
B.	B.
C.	C.
II. Dress	IV. Clothing
A.	A.
B.	B.
C.	C.

545. As children perform science experiments for the class, an outline may be made to show the main steps involved.

546. The children are given a copy of a well-known story. A group of children are asked to work together and make an outline of the events in the story.

For example:

> *Snow White* may be organized as follows:
>
> I. The king's family
>   A.
>   B.
>   C.
>
> II. The queen's desires
>   A.
>   B.
>
> III. Her serfs' tasks
>
> IV. Snow White's forest friends
>   A.
>   B.
>   C.
>   D.
>   E.
>   F.
>   G.
>
> V. The wicked queen's plan
>
> VI. Snow White's fate
>   A.
>   B.

547. Under the teacher's guidance, the children make a modified outline consisting of a horizontal line divided into sections by vertical lines placed at regular intervals. After a selection has been read, the main topics are discussed and the outline completed, using the children's ideas. Later, the children may make individual outlines of their own.

Example:

After a selection has been read concerning penguins and their habits, the following outline may be worked up:

PENGUINS

Location	Fur	Habits	Food
South Pole.	Black and white. After one year old, black and white with orange on the side of their heads.	Go to Pole to lay eggs. Fathers guard while mothers return for food. Form line of resistance against wind.	Found in water. Eat a lot, then go to Pole to lay eggs. Go without food for a long time— about two months.

Chapter Nine

TIDBITS AND LEFTOVERS

In a collection of activities such as this, there are always ideas that do not seem to fit into any particular skill area. These would include activities for special holidays, seasons, codes and the like.

548. Help the mailman sort his mail by sorting names and common nicknames for each piece of mail.

Henry
John
William
Robert
Margaret
Patricia
Elizabeth
Ronald

549. Arrange the names of your students in such a way that a message can be read down the middle. Omit the message so students may complete it. This can be used as a holiday puzzle.

Nicknames

Henry
John
William
Robert
Margaret
Patricia
Elizabeth
Ronald

Bob
Betty
Ronnie
Patsy
Bill
Hank
Maggie
Jack

550. Rule of Thumb. Children often have difficulty choosing a book that is on a suitable reading level. Prepare and display a chart with the following directions:

1. Choose a book that interests you.
2. Turn to page 5. Read it.
3. Hold up a finger for every word you don't know. If you must use your thumb (for five unknown words), the book may be hard for you.
4. If you have to use four fingers or less, try several pages in different parts of the book.
5. If you do not use your thumb on more than one page, CHECK IT OUT.

551. If you are using a basal reading book containing unrelated stories, it is not necessary to read them in sequence. You may stimulate interest by letting the group select the next story to be read.

552. Give each student a duplicated copy of a form similar to the following, in which a word is written vertically, one letter beneath another. On the left side, the word is written correctly; on the right, the spelling is backward.

a	t
p	n
a	e
r	m
t	t
m	r
e	a
n	p
t	a

Instruct the children to think of words beginning and ending with the letters opposite each other, and to write the words between the letters. For example, the first word might be **ant** or **announcement**. The first child to finish, with proper words, is the winner.

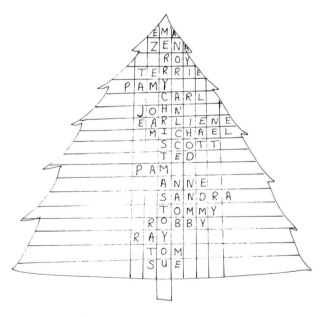

553. Let students make as many words as possible from the letters in the word **airplane.** They may use a letter only as many times as it appears in the given word. The letter or letters can be used over again when making a new word.

AIRPLANE

air	plane	plan
rip	lip	plain
rail	April	pan

To make the activity more difficult, seasonal, technical or multi-syllabic words containing several vowels can be employed.

Example:

SUPERCONDUCTIVITY

cone	once	nice
cope	ripe	under
pond	conduct	nurse
visit	dirty	evict

554. Make matching cards by cutting a rectangle from poster paper. Divide the top and bottom of the card into six equal sections. Words or pictures are placed on the top row, with the corresponding answers on the bottom. Punch holes in each section. Using string or yarn, the child matches the correct response from the top row to the bottom.

VARIATION: This activity may be used for math, language arts, science, social studies or as an aid in visual-motor development.

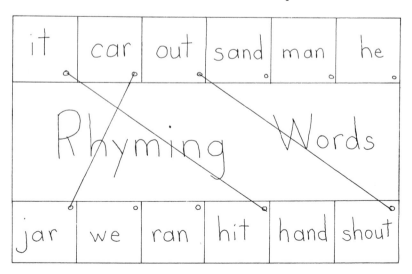

555. Write words as though you can hear them as well as see them. Think of the sound representation they may convey. For example, the word **slender** may be written with narrow lines to represent meaning connotation. Give the children a feeling for sound representation by having them express words in this creative manner.

556. Spelling Relay. Divide the class into two teams. The teacher reads a spelling word, a sound or a word containing a sound being studied. This is the signal to begin. The first two children must hop, skip or walk to the board, write the word or sound called and return to the end of their line. When both have returned, the next two children are given their turn. The line writing the most correctly spelled words, or sounds, is the winning team.

557. *Hint:* A handy card holder may be made from a piece of large poster board or oaktag. If oaktag is used, the rows may be made by pleating the paper accordion-style and stapling the edges. The edges may be trimmed with colored tape. If poster board is used, make the rows by cutting strips of paper and taping them in place with colored tape. The strips may be cut from the same colored poster board to make a neat appearance. This may be used for vocabulary practice or as an independent activity, having the child form sentences from experience stories. A smaller version of this activity may be used at students' desks for any variety of practice purposes. Card holders can be made from accordion-pleated paper.

558. Measure each child, and mark his height on a wall or bulletin board. Indicate each child's name. Encourage pupils to make comparisons as to who is shorter or taller, or how many are of the same height. Comparisons may be recorded as a pictorial graph, or the results written as a class story chart.

559. Records of personal experiences or group projects may be kept in diary form. Organizing material and ideas into this form makes it easy to add information from day to day. After a diary is kept for some kind of class project, the teacher can encourage students to keep reports of personal experiences in diaries of their own. These may be kept at school or at home. If the diaries are to be shared, this may be done as a small group activity. With young children, picture diaries may be kept. A tape line and scales may be kept in the room, and children can keep a monthly growth record to include in their personal diaries.

560. Write a short story: the first word beginning with **a,** the second with **b** and so forth, throughout the entire alphabet. The sentences in the story must make sense, and letter order must be maintained.

Example:

A boy came down every Friday.

561. Assorted ads from newspapers may be used as a unique method for developing skills in reading comprehension and locating information. Paste several ads on a piece of paper. On a separate sheet, write questions that can be answered from the ads. Let students study the ads and locate information needed to answer the questions. An answer sheet should also be made. All three sheets may be kept together in a folder.

VARIATION: The yellow pages of a telephone directory are excellent sources for ads.

562. Words are placed on cutouts representing the shapes of objects connected with various seasons of the year. Use seasonal vocabulary as well as other words. From the devices used, the child pulls out the words that do not apply to them.

563. Using familiar melodies, students make up creative poems to fit the rhythms of the songs.

564. Use the pictures from old greeting cards as a basis for mathematical story problems. Write the problems on the backs of the cards. Number the cards, and make an answer sheet for independent checking.

565. A "bookworm" may be used to keep a list of the books read by each child. Circles are cut from colored construction paper, and each child makes one to resemble the worm's head. On assorted colored circles, he writes the name and author of each book he has read. The circles are overlapped to form the worm, which may be hung up along the wall or as a bulletin board.

VARIATION: Make a large worm, with one section for each child. A slit is made at the top of each section. The children list books they have read on the inside of a folded piece of construction paper. Each child's name is written on the outside of his list. Make the list of an appropriate size so as to be easily removed from the worm to add new books.

566. The tachistoscope is useful in developing quick word recognition. A simple one may be made by cutting a piece of oaktag or cardboard

Make the basic shape
of a turkey with
detachable feathers.

to a convenient size (6″x8″). Fold back each of the long sides about one inch, to provide a tray for printed materials being used. An opening is cut in the center, wide enough to allow for the usual size of printed material. Another piece of oaktag or cardboard is attached as a shutter. Words are printed on separate cards and slipped into the fold on the underneath side. The words are slipped into place with the shutter closed. Each word is briefly exposed (five to ten seconds). The child recalls the word. If he is unable to give the word, open the shutter again so that he may study the word more carefully.

Another type of tachistoscope is made from a folded sheet of oaktag. Fold a 10″x8″ piece of paper in half so that the measurements will be five inches wide and eight inches long. Tape the eight-inch edges together. In one thickness of the oaktag, cut a window 2″x4″. The child views the practice word through this opening. Several words may be written on the same practice card. Be sure that proper spacing is allowed, so that only one word will appear in the window at a time. The practice card should be four and one-half inches wide, to allow sufficient room for sliding the word cards through the tachistoscope. This is a convenient and helpful aid for individual practice with rhyming, problem words or word families.

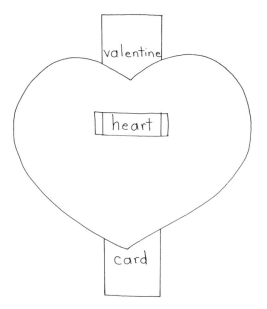

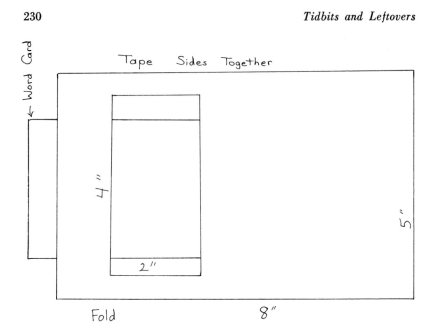

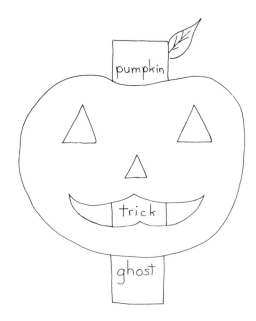

567. Using an exercise or story already on the board, dismiss the children by having them locate given things in the sentences. You may let them find the part asked for, erase it and line up at the door for play period, lunch or class dismissal.

Sample questions:

Find a compound word
Find a root word with a prefix
Find a four-syllable word
Find a given phoneme
Erase all the capital letters

568. Assign a number to each letter of the alphabet. Under each letter, write its corresponding number: under **A,** write 1; and under **Z,** write 26. Messages in number code are printed on the board, leaving spaces to separate words. The children will enjoy decoding and writing messages.

Examples:

1. 9–20   9–19   20–9–13–5   6–15–18   12–21–14–3–8.
   (It is time for lunch.)
2. 6–15–15–20–2–1–12–12   9–19   13–25   6–1–22–15–18–9–
   20–5   19–16–15–18–20.   (Football is my favorite sport.)

569. Rip stories from old readers and bind them to make reading booklets. A different colored cover may be used to designate each level. Comprehension question cards may be inserted in the inside covers. Pictures mounted on the front of each booklet add excitement and interest. These booklets are especially useful in science and social studies, when students may need easier reading material than the grade-level text.

570. Use a "reading house" to record books read by the students. The outline of a house is made on a large piece of cardboard. As a child completes a book, the title is printed on a brick, with his name at the bottom; the brick is then placed on the house. It is interesting to see how fast the house can be built by reading books. This same sort of thing may be done with a log cabin or a space rocket.

571. Proverbs and titles may be rewritten by the teacher. The students locate the correct answers by using the dictionary. Students are encouraged to rewrite proverbs on their own and have the others guess them.

Example:

Proverb: "A stitch in time saves nine."

A small tear repaired immediately will save a large patch later.

CROSS-INDEX OF ACTIVITIES

SKILL	ACTIVITY NUMBER
Abbreviations	374, 375, 548
Accent	215, 216
Alphabetizing	61, 132, 133, 139, 287, 290, 345, 346, 347, 348, 349, 350, 351, 352, 353, 354, 355, 357, 358, 359, 360, 361, 362, 380, 409, 568
Antonyms	304, 307, 310, 311, 312
Auditory Skills	49, 50, 51, 52, 53, 54, 55, 56, 98, 110, 132, 154, 156, 167, 174, 184, 185, 186, 190, 191, 195, 263, 336, 510, 521
Card Catalog	378, 379, 380
Classification— Categorizing Words	34, 142, 173, 181, 195, 246, 282, 283, 284, 285, 286, 287, 288, 289, 290, 291, 292, 293, 294, 295, 296, 297, 299, 300, 301, 303, 319, 328, 349, 385, 421, 423
Compound Words	83, 89, 90, 91, 130

234

Cross-Index of Activities

SKILL	ACTIVITY NUMBER
Consonant Blends	77, 110, 125, 126, 128, 129, 130, 131, 146, 147, 149, 150, 151, 152, 155, 157, 166, 174, 200
Contextual Analysis	78, 141, 161, 181, 201, 215, 247, 248, 249, 250, 251, 252, 253, 254, 255, 256, 257, 258, 259, 260, 261, 263, 325, 330, 332, 373, 512
Contractions	207, 208, 209
Creative Writing	100, 101, 105, 108, 111, 112, 113, 114, 115, 116, 117, 118, 119, 120, 165, 196, 251, 276, 317, 327, 493, 509, 559, 560
Descriptive Words	333, 334, 335, 336, 337, 338, 340, 341, 342, 343, 344, 461, 467
Details and Facts	102, 320, 328, 389, 417, 435, 436, 437, 438, 439, 440, 442, 443, 444, 445, 455, 458, 463, 464, 465, 466, 497, 498, 507, 508, 509, 510, 511, 519
Dictionary Skills	216, 257, 282, 284, 299, 300, 308, 313, 314, 320, 350, 354, 356, 363, 364, 365, 366, 367, 368, 369, 370, 371, 372, 373, 374, 375
Digraphs	110, 145, 147, 149, 150, 152, 153, 155, 174, 200
Directionality	92, 93, 94, 95, 96
Drawing Conclusions	98, 120, 456, 457, 458, 459, 460, 462, 465, 466, 473, 496, 497, 511, 513, 519, 522, 523, 524, 529
Experience Charts	100, 107, 108, 109, 110, 111, 114, 116, 290, 327, 559, 560
Final Consonants	110, 126, 143, 157, 166, 167, 168, 170, 171, 199, 203, 204, 205, 206, 249
Following Written Directions	74, 83, 85, 288, 291, 355, 436, 446, 447, 448, 449, 450, 451, 452, 453, 454, 455, 459, 517

SKILL	ACTIVITY NUMBER
Graphs and Charts	327, 404, 418, 419, 420, 421, 422, 423, 424, 425, 426, 427, 506, 558
Homonyms	215, 304, 305, 306, 313, 314
Index	350, 354, 386, 387, 388, 389, 390
Initial Consonants	110, 121, 122, 123, 124, 125, 126, 127, 128, 129, 132, 133, 134, 135, 136, 137, 138, 139, 142, 143, 144, 146, 157, 166, 168, 169, 170, 171, 187, 199, 200, 204, 206, 249, 251
Interpretation and Dramatization	101, 104, 105, 107, 109, 115, 116, 118, 120, 188, 267, 276, 277, 278, 279, 281, 335, 336, 392, 434, 468, 469, 470, 471, 472, 474, 476, 477, 478, 479, 480, 481, 483, 484, 485, 495
Letter Recognition	43, 57, 58, 59, 60, 61, 62, 63, 133, 136, 142, 174
Map and Globe Skills	397, 398, 399, 400, 401, 402, 403, 404, 405, 406, 407, 408, 409, 410, 411, 412, 413, 414, 415, 416, 417, 425
Oral Communication	12, 81, 96, 98, 99, 100, 101, 104, 107, 108, 110, 113, 116, 196, 232, 267, 268, 271, 274, 275, 276, 277, 278, 279, 280, 281, 338, 403, 468, 472, 475, 491, 492, 493, 494, 515
Outlining	396, 490, 515, 521, 541, 542, 543, 544, 545, 546, 547
Phonograms	85, 131, 140, 148, 154, 157, 166, 169, 179, 184, 185, 186, 188, 189, 190, 191, 192, 195, 197, 198, 199, 200, 201

SKILL	ACTIVITY NUMBER
Plurals	210, 211, 212, 221, 268
Rate Improvement	104, 280, 493, 500, 501, 502, 503, 504, 505, 506, 563, 566
Reference Books	381, 382, 383, 384, 385, 391, 393, 394, 395, 396, 406, 415, 419, 430, 467, 538
Rhyming Words	71, 76, 77, 124, 130, 138, 140, 184, 185, 186, 187, 188, 189, 190, 191, 192, 193, 194, 196, 197, 198, 199, 201, 202, 248, 439
Root Words, Prefixes, Suffixes	71, 143, 168, 171, 214, 217, 218, 219, 220, 221, 222, 223, 224, 225, 226, 227, 228, 229, 230, 231, 232, 233, 234, 235, 236, 237, 238, 246
Sentence Structure	79, 105, 113, 120, 209, 262, 264, 265, 266, 267, 268, 269, 271, 272, 293, 319, 324, 333, 334, 339, 344
Sequence of Events	94, 96, 97, 99, 448, 473, 490, 526, 527, 528, 529, 530, 531, 532, 533, 534, 535, 536, 537, 538
Sharing Books	396, 478, 479, 480, 482, 483, 484, 485, 486, 487, 488, 489, 490, 491, 492, 565
Silent Letters	164, 175, 176, 177, 178, 205
Summarizing	105, 119, 395, 432, 433, 434, 486, 499, 539, 540, 547
Syllabication	159, 172, 239, 240, 241, 242, 243, 244, 245, 246
Synonyms	304, 307, 308
Table of Contents, Preface	376, 377
Tables	428, 429, 430, 431
Topic and Summary Sentences and Words	270, 390, 433, 514, 516, 517, 518, 520, 521, 539, 540

SKILL	ACTIVITY NUMBER
Visual Discrimination	6, 9, 10, 12, 13, 19, 28, 29, 30, 31, 32, 33, 34, 35, 36, 37, 38, 39, 40, 41, 42, 43, 44, 45, 46, 47, 48, 58, 59, 62, 64, 65, 66, 67, 68, 69, 70, 75, 103, 113, 153, 154, 174, 324
Visual Skills	1, 2, 3, 4, 5, 6, 7, 8, 9, 10, 12, 16, 37, 78, 87, 102
Visual-Motor Skills	1, 7, 11, 13, 14, 15, 16, 17, 18, 19, 20, 21, 22, 23, 24, 25, 26, 27, 32, 35, 37, 39, 40, 41, 52, 60, 62, 123, 138, 147, 187, 348, 554
Vocabulary (Sight and Meaning)	66, 78, 81, 82, 86, 89, 90, 91, 127, 134, 139, 142, 144, 173, 181, 185, 195, 213, 225, 233, 246, 254, 255, 282, 289, 297, 298, 302, 309, 316, 318, 321, 322, 323, 326, 330, 331, 332, 342, 552, 553, 557
Vowels, Vowel Digraphs and Diphthongs	137, 140, 156, 157, 158, 159, 160, 161, 162, 163, 164, 165, 170, 171, 175, 176, 178, 179, 180, 181, 182, 202, 261, 366
Vowels with **R**	159, 179, 183, 187, 193
Word Recognition	5, 43, 45, 63, 66, 67, 68, 69, 70, 71, 72, 73, 74, 75, 76, 77, 78, 80, 83, 84, 86, 129, 213, 243, 252, 258, 563, 566